Great Writing 4

Great Essays

Great Writing 4

Great Essays

THIRD EDITION

KEITH S. FOLSE
UNIVERSITY OF CENTRAL FLORIDA

APRIL MUCHMORE-VOKOUN
HILLSBOROUGH COMMUNITY COLLEGE

ELENA VESTRI SOLOMON
EMIRATES COLLEGE FOR ADVANCED EDUCATION
UAE

HEINLE
CENGAGE Learning™

Australia • Canada • Mexico • Singapore • Spain • United Kingdom • United States

HEINLE
CENGAGE Learning

Great Writing 4: Great Essays, Third Edition

Keith S. Folse, April Muchmore-Vokoun, Elena Vestri Solomon

Publisher: Sherrise Roehr

Acquisition Editor: Tom Jefferies

Senior Development Editor: Yeny Kim

Assistant Editor: Marissa Petrarca

Director of Content and Media Production: Michael Burggren

Marketing Director, U.S.: Jim McDonough

Director of Adult Education Sales: Eric Bredenberg

Marketing Communications Manager: Beth Leonard

Senior Product Marketing Manager: Katie Kelley

Academic Marketing Manager: Caitlin Driscoll

Senior Content Project Manager: Maryellen Eschmann-Killeen

Senior Print Buyer: Susan Spencer

Composition: Pre-Press PMG

Library of Congress Control Number: 2009926619

ISBN-13: 978-1-4240-5101-4

ISBN-10: 1-4240-5101-0

Heinle, Cengage Learning
20 Channel Center Street
Boston, MA 02210
USA

Cengage learning is a leading provider of customized learning solutions with office locations around the globe, including Singapore, the United Kingdom, Australia, Mexico, Brazil, and Japan. Locate our local office at: **International. cengage.com/region**

Cengage Learning products are represented in Canada by Nelson Education, Ltd.

Visit Heinle online at **elt.heinle.com**
Visit out corporate website at **cengage.com**

Printed in the United States of America
1 2 3 4 5 6 7 13 12 11 10 09

Contents

Overview

Great Writing 4: Great Essays is the fourth book in the five-level *Great Writing* series of composition books. *Great Writing 4* provides introductory instruction and extensive practical exercises and activities in essay writing at the high-intermediate and advanced levels. This book contains a wide variety of exercises that offer practice in both working with the writing process and developing a final written product. We assume that students can write good paragraphs and that what they need is instruction in, modeling of, and guidance with writing essays.

There are as many ways to write essays as there are writers. Essay writing reflects a writer's knowledge of essay conventions as much as it reflects the writer's creativity. Thus, essay writing is both a science and an art. Since no art form can be "taught" precisely, this book offers models of good academic essays as the basic level of essay writing from which students produce their own essays. We realize that some students may not go beyond the level of the examples whereas other students may advance in their essay writing.

In this latest edition of *Great Writing 4,* we have made a conscious effort to include a wide array of writing activities representing varying approaches to the teaching of writing. Although we realize that few writing teachers are completely satisfied with any writing text, we believe that within this variety of activities and approaches, most teachers will find what their students need in order to improve writing skills, presented in a way that is compatible with how teachers think ESL writing ought to be taught. Also new to this edition are vocabulary activities designed to enhance students' word association skills and use of collocations. Vocabulary mastery is a key ingredient in developing advanced writing skills.

We have designed this book for high-intermediate to advanced students. Depending on the class level and the amount of writing that is done outside of class hours, there is enough material for 60 to 80 classroom hours. Provided that enough writing is done outside of the classroom, the number of classroom instruction hours can be as little as 40.

Some of the highlights of *Great Writing 4* include the following:

- **Abundance of activities and writing practice** We have made every effort to include more than enough writing instruction and practice to eliminate the need for excessive ancillary materials. The new third edition contains 120 activities, including 25 suggestions for additional essay writing assignments. New to this edition, each unit contains a section focusing on timed writing. In addition, the Brief Writer's Handbook with Activities and the Appendices contain supplementary practice in language usage and grammar. Most of these activities and practice exercises are based on the 22 full-length example essays found throughout the text.

- **Step-by-step instruction** Some English learners are already good writers in their native language. *Great Writing 4* will allow these students to study the different rhetorical styles commonly used in English writing. Other students need work in the basic steps involved in the process of composing an essay. These students in particular will benefit from the step-by-step activities in *Great Writing 4*. Of special interest are Appendix 1, Building Better Sentences, which contains guided activities to improve students' sentence combination skills, and the new Editing Your Writing section of the Brief Writer's Handbook with Activities, which provides a step-by-step introduction to the process of identifying and correcting errors and rewriting drafts based on teacher feedback.

- **Contextualized activities** An important feature of *Great Writing 4* is the inclusion of 22 example essays distributed throughout the units. Many of the activities in this book are presented in the context of these example essays. This provides learners with more input in English composition and essay organization and cohesion.

- **Enhanced focus on vocabulary** A piece of writing is often only as good as the writer's ability to use a wide range of appropriate vocabulary. To help our learners achieve this important goal, this third edition includes more emphasis on vocabulary in six key ways:

    1. *More vocabulary items.* We have revised some of the essays to include more words that will help students improve their own writing.

    2. *More glossing.* We have glossed more vocabulary items after the essays.

    3. *More recycling.* We have intentionally recycled vocabulary items from unit to unit. With increased exposure, students will learn not only the basic meanings of words and phrases, but also acquire actual natural usage.

    4. *Practice of meaning.* New to this edition, each unit contains a Word Associations activity that allows students to check their understanding of the basic meaning of new vocabulary.

    5. *Practice of collocations.* Also new to this third edition, each unit includes an activity on collocations, which are words or groups of words that naturally and frequently co-occur with a target word. Learning collocations will help students build on their bank of commonly used phrases, which is the first step to incorporating those phrases into their writing.

    6. *Active use of vocabulary.* While knowing word meanings may allow for passive recognition in reading or listening, it is often insufficient for actual use in writing (or speaking). Students need to practice these vocabulary items and collocations in their writing. To this end, students are instructed to use some of the vocabulary items presented in the vocabulary activities as they complete the end-of-unit assignment of writing an essay in the rhetorical style covered in the unit.

- **Focus on quality** Composing an essay involves both a process and a product. All English learners are rightfully concerned about their written products. For many students, not being able to write effectively and easily in English is a major obstacle to their educational plans. Thus, the quality of any written work is important. To this end, the activities in this book deal with elements that affect the quality of a written product, including grammar, organization, and logic. Although in this text there is information about both process and product in essay writing, it should be noted that the focus is slightly more on the final written product. In addition, the Brief Writer's Handbook with Activities contains supplementary instruction in several key writing components, including sentence types, grammar, and the use of connectors.

The best judge of which units and which activities should be covered with any group of students is always the teacher. It is up to you to gauge the needs of your students and then match these needs with the material in this book.

Text Organization

Great Writing 4 consists of two general sections. The first section consists of the five actual units that present the features of a good essay and four kinds of essay writing. The second section includes the Brief Writer's Handbook with Activities and the Appendices, which contain ancillary and additional practice material.

Units 1–5

This section begins by teaching, in general terms, how to construct a five-paragraph essay. Unit 1 presents the overall organization of an essay. It also offers some specific suggestions for writing the introduction of an essay, including how to write a good hook and a solid thesis statement. Students who are already familiar with the essay form may skip most of the material in Unit 1. Units 2 through 5 teach four different kinds of essays—narrative, comparison, cause-effect, and argumentative. These four essay types can be covered in any order.

Brief Writer's Handbook with Activities

The Brief Writer's Handbook with Activities offers additional support in both the process and the mechanics of writing.

Understanding the Writing Process: The Seven Steps explains the seven steps in the process of writing an essay and includes student examples for a few of the steps. Rather than merely listing the seven steps as many books do, this section walks students through the step-by-step process.

New to this edition, the **Editing Your Writing** section guides students through the editing process. Teachers often spend considerable time marking and commenting on student work, but many students have difficulty incorporating teacher feedback as they write their next draft. While many textbooks offer general advice on editing, students often need more specific and explicit advice. This innovative section is meant to provide students with the step-by-step training they need to effectively integrate teacher feedback as they rewrite their drafts. In Editing Your Writing, students analyze three versions of the same student essay.

- Version 1 is an uncorrected draft of a student-generated timed writing assignment. Students read the assigned writing task and then the original essay to compare the task and the overall product. Students then read the essay for a closer inspection of the organization, grammar, vocabulary, and writing style.

- Version 2 is the same essay with instructor comments. In this version, students can see what the instructor has written. Students will see both positive and negative comments. An important point here is for students to compare their comments after reading Version 1 with the teacher's comments. Which comments are similar? Which areas are different?

- Version 3 is the second draft of the work after the teacher's comments. The writer has accepted some of the teacher's comments but appears to have rejected others, which is a very common occurrence in all composition classes. Through guided questions, students are asked to identify sections that were changed. Were the changes made in response to teacher comments, or were the changes original changes initiated by the student?

The **Sentence Types** section defines the three basic sentence types in English, provides examples, and reinforces the concepts through practice. The **Additional Grammar Activities** section provides supplementary practice in some of the most common grammatical problems for English learners in the context of paragraphs within whole essays. Many English learners see grammar as their biggest problem. While other writing needs often deserve more attention, students recognize that their ability to express themselves in English is limited by the level of their English proficiency. This section addresses this student need for additional grammar practice. The **Connectors** section contains a list of useful connectors that students can refer to as a resource for their writing, supplementing the Language Focus sections that deal with connectors within the units.

Citations and Plagiarism is new to this third edition, but what it addresses is not a new challenge: citing borrowed information in order to avoid plagiarism. In addition to the teaching notes within the units, we have included a separate section on citations and plagiarism. For many students, the notion of plagiarism is new. Many English learners find it difficult to paraphrase material because they either do not understand the original material well enough in the first place or they do not have enough vocabulary knowledge to express the same idea in their own words. Whether writers paraphrase or use an exact quote, they need to learn how to cite the borrowed information to avoid plagiarism.

Appendices

Appendix 1, Building Better Sentences, is dedicated to sentence-combining skills. Individual sentences taken from each of the example essays have been isolated and divided into short, choppy sentences that students are asked to combine into longer sentences. This type of activity hones students' skills in using prepositional phrases, coordinating conjunctions, conjunctive adverbs, and other transitional devices to write concise sentences. After completing the exercises, students are able to check their written products with the original sentences found in the example essays.

In Appendix 2, you will find peer editing sheets for students to use when they read each other's work and offer feedback. For each essay type, there is a peer editing sheet for the outline and another for the essay. We believe that asking a student to comment on another student's writing without guidance is poor pedagogy and may result in hurt feelings for the writer. Not everyone is a good writer; therefore, we cannot assume that a less capable writer is able to make useful comments on a better writer's paper. Likewise, not all good writers know how to guide weaker writers toward an improved essay. These peer editing sheets provide structure and focused guidance to help everyone make useful comments. For those students who are able to go beyond the basics, several of the questions are open-ended and invite additional comments.

Contents of a Unit

The common features of each unit are listed below. Although each unit has a specific writing goal and language focus (listed at the beginning of the unit), the following features appear in every unit.

Example Essays

Because we believe that writing and reading are inextricably related, the example essays are often preceded by short schema-building questions for small groups or the whole class. The answers to these questions help students develop a mental image of the organization of the essay, which in turn helps students understand how rhetorical patterns can aid in overall reading comprehension. Potentially unfamiliar vocabulary is glossed. Example essays are usually followed by questions specifically constructed to focus learners' attention on organization, syntactic structures, or other essay features.

Writer's Notes

Rather than large boxed areas of teaching overflowing with information, *Great Writing 4* features small chunks of writing advice under this heading. The content of these notes varies from brainstorming techniques, to peer editing guidelines, to hints for generating supporting details, to plagiarism.

Language Focus

This section focuses students' attention on word-level details that we believe are important to the kind of essay featured in the unit. If students work with different writing devices, such as connectors, they will be better equipped to use them in their own writing. Those students who need more practice should work through any related additional practices in the "Additional Grammar Activities" section of the Brief Writer's Handbook with Activities.

Building Better Vocabulary

In this section, which is new to this edition, students will complete two vocabulary-building activities. In these activities, vocabulary words have been taken from each unit's writing, and special attention is paid to building schema and collocations. In the first activity, Word Associations, the students identify words that best relate to the target vocabulary word. This allows them to build connections to more words and thus grow their vocabulary more quickly. The second activity, Using Collocations, builds students' understanding that some words typically appear in conjunction with a certain word or phrase. This knowledge helps students learn these specific word combinations, or collocations.

Building Better Sentences

After every example essay read, students are asked to turn to Appendix 1 and work on building better sentences. This activity focuses on students' sentence-level writing skills using content from the example essays. For those students who lack confidence in producing longer or more complicated sentences, this type of activity concentrates on the manipulation of words and ideas on the sentence level.

Completing an Outline

In each unit, students are asked to read partial outlines and fill in the missing pieces. This strategy will help develop students' organizational skills in providing appropriate supporting details and in organizing ideas within an essay.

Completing an Sample Essay

In Units 2 through 5, students are asked to fill in the missing supporting details in a partial essay, which is a reinforcement of the model presented earlier in the unit. We designed this activity to give further practice in writing supporting sentences in paragraphs.

Analyzing an Essay

For each essay type, students using *Great Writing 4* are asked to read an essay and answer questions that focus on various aspects of writing at the high-intermediate to advanced levels, such as recognizing the topic sentence, identifying the use of examples as support, or discovering the writer's purpose for including certain information.

Topics for Writing

Each unit ends with an assignment to write an essay in the rhetorical style covered in the unit. For further practice, we include a list of five additional writing ideas in each unit.

Timed Writing

One way to improve student comfort with the task of writing under a deadline, such as during a testing situation, is to provide them with numerous writing opportunities while being timed. As a result, in this third edition, the final activity in each unit features a timed writing assignment. This assignment can be done alone or in conjunction with the editing approach introduced in the Editing Your Work section of the Brief Writer's Handbook. Students are given a writing prompt and guidelines. Students are then given five minutes to brainstorm ideas about the topic or create a brief outline, followed by forty minutes to write their essay.

Although we have placed this Timed Writing as a final task within a unit, some teachers may prefer to assign this topic as the first task of the unit. In this case, these teachers usually collect students' work and then have them rewrite it at the end of the unit. In this way, students have two opportunities to practice composition while teachers only read and mark papers once.

Peer Editing

In these activities, student partners offer each other written suggestions for improving their essays. Just as students have different writing abilities, they also have different editing abilities. For this reason, we believe that students benefit from guided peer editing. After students write an outline, they can use the peer editing sheet for outlines, which addresses content and organization. Students can receive valuable advice from each other regarding thesis statements, topic sentences, supporting information, and logic before writing the essay. The second peer editing activity is for the essay. Pairs of students exchange their completed essays and offer written comments, using the peer editing sheet. We recommend that students spend 15 to 20 minutes reading a classmate's essay and writing comments according to the questions on the peer editing sheet. Since a certain amount of trust and cooperation is involved in peer editing, it is important to make sure that students work with peers they feel compatible with.

About the Activities and Practices

Teachers have long noticed that students often do well with grammar in discrete sentences but may have problems with the same grammar when it occurs in an essay. Consequently, most of the activities and practices in *Great Writing 4* work with complete essays or focus on one paragraph within an essay. For example, instead of several unrelated sentences for practice with connectors, a complete essay is given to work with. Our hope is that by practicing the grammatical problem in the target medium, students will produce more accurate writing sooner.

The earliest ESL composition textbooks were merely extensions of ESL grammar classes. The activities in these books did not practice English composition as much as they did ESL grammar points. Later books, on the other hand, tended to focus too much on the composing process. We feel that this focus ignores the important fact that the real goals of our English learners are both to produce a presentable product and to master the composing process. From our years of ESL and other L2 teaching experience, we believe that *Great Writing 4* allows English learners to achieve both of these goals.

For the answer key, additional exercises, and other instructor resources, visit the *Great Writing 4* instructor Web site at elt.heinle.com/greatwriting.

Additional exercises for each unit are available to students on the *Great Writing 4* student Web site at elt.heinle.com/greatwriting.

Acknowledgments

We would like to thank ESL and English composition colleagues who have generously shared their ideas, insights, and feedback on L2 writing, university English course requirements, and textbook design. In addition, we would like to thank teachers on two electronic lists, TESL-L and TESLIE-L, who responded to our queries and thereby helped us write this book.

We would like to thank our editors at Heinle/Cengage Learning, Thomas Jefferies and Yeny Kim. We also remain forever grateful to our previous editors at Houghton Mifflin, Susan Maguire, Kathy Sands-Boehmer, and Kathleen Smith, for their indispensable guidance throughout the birth and growth of this writing project. We are grateful to Joann Kozyrev and Anna Rice at Houghton Mifflin for their enthusiastic support of our work.

Likewise, we are indebted to the following reviewers who offered ideas and suggestions that shaped our revisions:

Don Beck, The University of Findlay, OH
Len Chen, Palomar College, CA
Pauline Chu, Long Island Business Institute, NY
Gretchen Mack, Community College of Denver, CO
Nick Hilmers, DePaul University, IL
Gloria Huang, DePaul University, IL
Danielle Pelletier, Northeastern University, MA
Christine Tierney, Houston Community College, TX

Finally, many thanks go to our students who have taught us what ESL composition ought to be. Without them, this work would have been impossible.

Keith S. Folse
April Muchmore-Vokoun
Elena Vestri Solomon

Guided Tour

✳ NEW TO THIS EDITION

A new **four-color design** allows for engaging, easy to follow lessons.

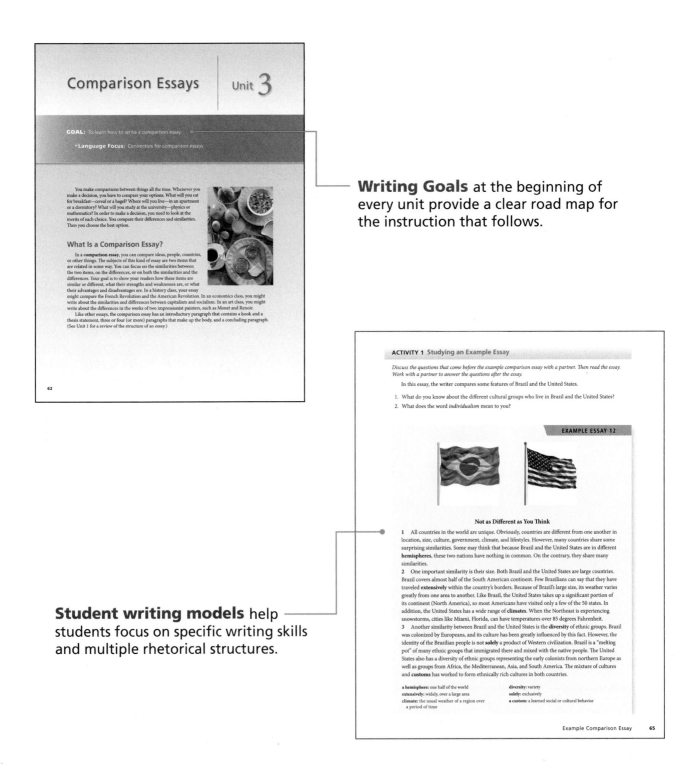

Writing Goals at the beginning of every unit provide a clear road map for the instruction that follows.

Student writing models help students focus on specific writing skills and multiple rhetorical structures.

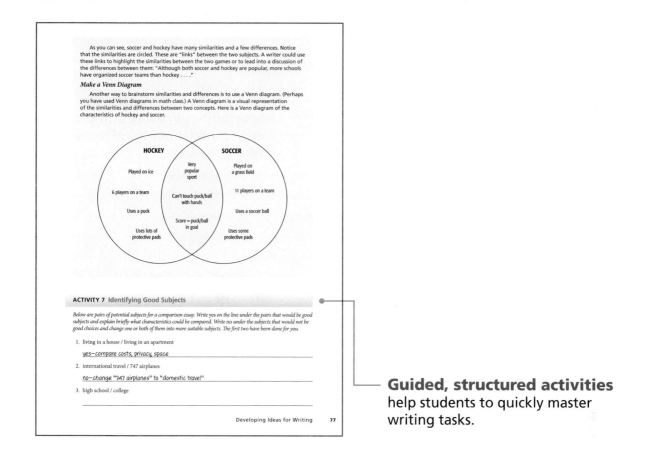

As you can see, soccer and hockey have many similarities and a few differences. Notice that the similarities are circled. These are "links" between the two subjects. A writer could use these links to highlight the similarities between the two games or to lead into a discussion of the differences between them: "Although both soccer and hockey are popular, more schools have organized soccer teams than hockey . . . ."

Make a Venn Diagram

Another way to brainstorm similarities and differences is to use a Venn diagram. (Perhaps you have used Venn diagrams in math class.) A Venn diagram is a visual representation of the similarities and differences between two concepts. Here is a Venn diagram of the characteristics of hockey and soccer.

ACTIVITY 7 Identifying Good Subjects

Below are pairs of potential subjects for a comparison essay. Write yes on the line under the pairs that would be good subjects and explain briefly what characteristics could be compared. Write no under the subjects that would not be good choices and change one or both of them into more suitable subjects. The first two have been done for you.

1. living in a house / living in an apartment

   yes—compare costs, privacy, space

2. international travel / 747 airplanes

   no—change "747 airplanes" to "domestic travel"

3. high school / college

Guided, structured activities help students to quickly master writing tasks.

4. the weather in Toronto / tourist attractions in Toronto

5. wild animals / animals in a zoo

6. computers / computer keyboards

7. hands / feet

8. the surface of the ocean floor / the surface of the continents

9. the Earth / the North American continent

10. Chinese food / Mexican food

For more practice with identifying subjects for comparison essays, try Unit 3, Activity 3 on the *Great Writing 4* Web site: elt.heinle.com/greatwriting

Writer's Note

Writing from Personal Experience

Many students like to compare and contrast certain features of their cultures to those of other cultures. These topics usually lead to interesting essays that engage readers.

Original Student Writing: Comparison Essay

ACTIVITY 8 Working with a Topic

Complete the following steps to develop ideas for a comparison essay.

1. Choose one topic from the list below or use your own idea for a topic. If you want to use an original idea, talk to your teacher to see if it is appropriate for a comparison essay.

two sports	two movies	two systems of education
two places	two machines	two kinds of professions
two desserts	two famous people	two celebrations or holidays

Writer's Note sections provide relevant writing-skill instruction that supports the unit's writing goals.

ACTIVITY 10 Peer Editing Your Outline

Exchange books with a partner and look at Activity 9. Read your partner's outline. Then use Peer Editing Sheet 3 on page 189 to help you comment on your partner's outline. Use your partner's feedback to revise your outline. Make sure you have enough information to develop your supporting sentences.

ACTIVITY 11 Writing a Comparison Essay

Write a comparison essay based on your revised outline from Activity 10. Use at least five of the vocabulary words or phrases presented in Activity 5 and Activity 6. Underline these words and phrases in your essay. Be sure to refer to the seven steps in the writing process in the Brief Writer's Handbook with Activities on pages 131–138.

ACTIVITY 12 Peer Editing Your Essay

Exchange papers from Activity 11 with a partner. Read your partner's writing. Then use Peer Editing Sheet 4 on page 191 to help you comment on your partner's writing. Be sure to offer positive suggestions and comments that will help your partner improve his or her writing. Consider your partner's comments as you revise your own writing.

Additional Topics for Writing

Here are more ideas for topics for a comparison essay. Before you write, be sure to refer to the seven steps in the writing process in the Brief Writer's Handbook with Activities, pages 131–138.

TOPIC 1: Compare a book to its movie version. How are the two similar and different? Are the characters and the plot the same? Do you like the movie or the book better? Explain your answer.

TOPIC 2: Compare the situation in a country before and after an important historical event, such as Cuba before and after Fidel Castro came to power.

TOPIC 3: Discuss two kinds of music, such as classical and pop. A few points of comparison might be artists, instruments, audiences, and popularity.

TOPIC 4: Show how the world has changed since the invention of the cell (mobile) phone. How did people communicate before its invention? How easy or difficult was it to get in contact with someone?

TOPIC 5: Show the similarities and differences in the ways that two cultures celebrate an important event, such as a birthday, wedding, or funeral.

Individual and peer **editing** opportunities in every unit provide focused guidelines for effective editing practice.

Suggestions for additional writing activities provide the opportunity for even more writing on a variety of topics.

Integrated **grammar** lessons teach and practice the grammar necessary to accomplish the writing goals of the unit.

Connectors That Show Contrast	
Between sentences or paragraphs	**Example**
However, / On the other hand,	Many differences are clear to even novice gardeners. **However / On the other hand,** some of their differences are not very obvious.
In contrast,	Red Beauty has a strong, sweet fragrance. **In contrast,** Midnight Dream's fragrance is light and fruity.
Although . . . ,	Both Midnight Dream roses and Red Beauty roses are red. **Although** both these two varieties have red flowers, Midnight Dream roses are much darker than Red Beauty roses.
Even though . . . ,	Red Beauty roses and Midnight Dream roses are long-stemmed roses. **Even though** both these two species are long-stemmed roses, Red Beauty stems are thin and covered with thorns while Midnight Dream stems are thick and have almost no thorns.
Unlike . . . ,	What do we know about the cost of these two kinds of roses? **Unlike** Red Beauty, Midnight Dream roses are relatively inexpensive.

ACTIVITY 4 Connectors

Read the following student essay and circle the appropriate connector in each set of parentheses. Refer to the list in the Language Focus section on pages 71–72, if necessary.

The writer in this essay compares the university entrance requirements in Taiwan before and after 2001 when educational reforms were implemented.

Building Better Vocabulary

ACTIVITY 5 Word Associations

Circle the word or phrase that is most closely related to the word or phrase on the left. If necessary, use a dictionary to check the meaning of words you do not know.

1. diversity	difference	distance
2. customs	shirts	traditions
3. a concept	an idea	music
4. remarkable	repetitive	amazing
5. a hemisphere	in math class	in geography class
6. to take root	to begin to grow	to refuse to grow
7. solely	hardly	only
8. sound	misunderstood	solid
9. likewise	but	also
10. a climate	weather	yearly salary

ACTIVITY 6 Using Collocations

Fill in each blank with the word on the left that most naturally completes the phrase on the right. If necessary, use a dictionary to check the meaning of words you do not know.

1. make / pay	to_____ attention to something
2. on / to	to be vital _____ (the plan's success)
3. origin / root	to take _____
4. find / reach	to _____ a decision
5. at / in	the differences _____ size, cost, and color
6. advantage / time	to take _____ of
7. superior / ultimate	our _____ goal
8. likewise / significant	a _____ portion
9. common / contrary	to have nothing in _____
10. groups / people	ethnic _____

✴ NEW TO THIS EDITION

Building Better Vocabulary sections teach students how to accurately and effectively use written English.

Timed Writing

How quickly can you write in English? There are many times when you must write quickly, such as on a test. It is important to feel comfortable during those times. Timed-writing practice can make you feel better about writing quickly in English.

First, read the essay guidelines below. Then take out a piece of paper. Read the writing prompt below the guidelines. As quickly as you can, write a basic outline for this writing prompt (including the thesis and your three main points). You should spend no more than 5 minutes on your outline.

You will then have 40 minutes to write a 5-paragraph comparison essay about your topic. At the end of the 40 minutes, your teacher will collect your work and return it to you at a later date.

Comparison Essay Guidelines

• Use the point-by-point method.
• Remember to give your essay a title.
• Double-space your essay.
• Write as legibly as possible (if you are not using a computer).
• Include a short introduction (with a thesis statement), three body paragraphs, and a conclusion.
• Try to give yourself a few minutes before the end of the activity to review your work. Check for spelling, verb tense, and subject-verb agreement mistakes.

Compare two popular vacation destinations.

✴ NEW TO THIS EDITION

Timed writing activities prepare students for success on standardized tests like the TOEFL®.

Supplements

✴ NEW TO THIS EDITION

The **Assessment CD-ROM with *ExamView*®** allows teachers to create tests and quizzes easily.

✴ NEW TO THIS EDITION

The **Classroom Presentation Tool** makes instruction clearer and learning simpler.

For **Instructor's Resources** like lesson-planning tips, please visit elt.heinle.com/greatwriting.

Exploring the Essay

GOAL: To learn about the structure of an essay

What Is an Essay?

Essays are everywhere—in books, magazines, newspapers, and other printed material. An **essay** is a short collection of paragraphs that presents facts, opinions, and ideas about a topic. Topics can range from a description of a visit to the beach to an argument for (or against) tax increases.

An essay usually has three to ten paragraphs. Most of the essays in this book have five or six paragraphs. Each paragraph discusses one idea, often stated in the topic sentence of the paragraph. This idea is related to the topic of the whole essay. The topic sentence of a paragraph can be located anywhere, but the most common place is at the beginning of the paragraph.

The following illustration shows how letters, words, sentences, paragraphs, and essays are related. Letters can be combined into a word. Words can be combined into a sentence. Sentences can be combined into a paragraph. Finally, paragraphs can be combined into an essay. In this book, you will study essays.

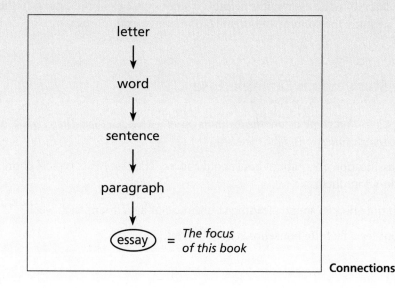

letter

↓

word

↓

sentence

↓

paragraph

↓

(essay) = *The focus of this book*

Connections

Kinds of Essays

There are many different ways to write an essay. The method that a writer chooses is often based on the topic of the essay. The writer needs to consider what kind of essay will convey his or her ideas in the clearest and most accurate way. In this book, you will learn about four common kinds of essays: **narrative**, **comparison**, **cause-effect**, and **argumentative**. Each of the next four units presents one of these kinds of essay writing.

It is important, however, to note here that many writers use more than one method within the same essay. For example, if you are comparing the lifestyles of actors and professional athletes, you might include information about how actors and professional athletes get their start in their careers (cause-effect). You might also give an account of a specific athlete's story (narrative). In addition, your essay could include facts and opinions about how one profession is more respected than the other (comparison and argumentative). It is likely that a good writer will use more than one kind of writing in an essay. Once you learn about these essay methods separately and become comfortable with them, you can experiment with weaving them together to produce well-written essays in English.

 For practice with identifying kinds of essays, try Unit 1, Activity 1 on the *Great Writing 4* Web site: elt.heinle.com/greatwriting

---

✏ Writer's Note

Parts of an Essay

Notice that an essay has three basic parts: the **introduction**, the **body**, and the **conclusion**. The introduction is the first paragraph, the conclusion is the last paragraph, and the body consists of the paragraphs in between. You will study these three parts later in this unit.

Example Essays

Before you learn to write essays, it is helpful to study some example essays. In the next five activities, you will read and study the content and organization of five example essays.

ACTIVITY 1 Studying an Example Essay

Discuss the questions that come before the example essay with a partner. Then read the essay. Work with a partner to answer the questions after the essay.

This is a classification essay about household chores. The essay lists typical chores and explains what the writer thinks about them.

1. How much time do you spend cleaning your house or apartment each week?

2. What is your least favorite household chore? Why?

Cinderella and Her <u>Odious</u> <u>Household</u> <u>Chores</u>

1   Almost everyone knows how the story of Cinderella ends, but do people actually think about how she spent her days before she met the prince? Her daily **routine** was not glamorous. She did everything from sweeping the floors to cooking the meals. If someone had asked Cinderella which chores she did not particularly like, she probably would have answered, "Why, none, of course. Housework is my duty!" In today's increasingly busy society, however, most people admit that they have definite dislikes for certain household chores. The top three of these unpopular tasks often include ironing clothes, washing dishes, and cleaning the bathroom.

2   One of the most hated chores for many people is ironing clothes because it is not a task that can be completed quickly or thoughtlessly. Each piece of clothing must be handled individually, so ironing a basket of laundry can take hours! After ironing a piece of clothing **meticulously**, which **entails** smoothing out the fabric, following the seams, and getting the creases just right, it needs to be put on a hanger as soon as possible. If not, this item might become **wrinkled** and need to be ironed again. Perhaps the reason that ironing is not a favorite chore is that it requires extreme attention to detail from beginning to end.

3   Another household chore that many people dislike is washing dishes. Of course, some people claim that this chore is no longer a problem because dishwashers are available now! However, no one would argue that dishes, **silverware**, and especially pots and pans washed in a dishwasher come out as clean as they do when washed by hand. For this reason, many people continue to wash their dishes by hand, but they are not necessarily happy doing it. Washing dishes is a dirty job that requires not only **elbow grease** to scrape food off the dishes but also patience to rinse and dry them. In addition, unlike ironing clothes, washing dishes is a chore that usually must be done every day. Regardless of how Cinderella felt about this particular chore, it is obvious that most people do not enjoy doing it.

4   Although ironing clothes and washing dishes are not the most pleasant household chores, perhaps the most **dreaded** chore is cleaning the bathroom. This task involves **tackling** three main areas: the bathtub, sink, and toilet. Because the bathroom is full of germs, a quick wiping of the surfaces is often not enough. As a result, strong bathroom cleansers are necessary to clean and **disinfect** this room. The task of cleaning the bathroom is so unpleasant that some people wear rubber gloves when they attempt it. The only positive point about cleaning the bathroom is that it does not have to be done on a daily basis.

odious: very unpleasant
household: referring to the house
a chore: a specific task or job, usually done in the home
a routine: a set of actions done regularly
meticulously: thoroughly and carefully
entail: to include
wrinkled: having an unwanted line or crease

silverware: eating utensils, such as forks, knives, and spoons
elbow grease: physical strength, usually using the hands
dreaded: feared
tackle: to undertake, begin
disinfect: to purify, eliminate germs

5   Maintaining a house means doing a wide variety of unpleasant chores. Cinderella knew this, and so does the rest of the world. Many individuals do not always have the luxury of hiring an outside person to do their own housework, so they must **make do** with their own resources. Still, taking pride in the results of this hard work helps many people get through the unpleasantness of these chores.

make do: to manage with what is available

3. According to the author of this essay, what are the three least popular household chores?

_____   _____   _____

Writer's Note

The Hook

The opening sentence of any essay is called the **hook**. A hook in writing is used to "catch" readers' attention and grab their interest so that they will want to read the essay. (See pages 20–21 for more information about hooks.)

4. In a few words, describe the hook of this essay. _____

_____

5. Do you think this hook is effective? Does it grab your attention? Why or why not?

_____

_____

6. How many paragraphs does this essay have? _____ Which paragraph is the introduction? _____

Which paragraph is the conclusion? _____ Which paragraphs make up the body? _____

7. In a few words, what is the general topic of this essay? _____

_____

8. Can you find a sentence in Paragraph 1 that tells readers what to expect in Paragraphs 2, 3, and 4?

Write that sentence here. _____

_____

Writer's Note

The Thesis Statement

In "Cinderella and Her Odious Household Chores," the last sentence in Paragraph 1 is the **thesis statement**. It states the main idea of the essay and tells what the organization of the information will be. (See page 22 for more information about thesis statements.)

9. What is the main idea of Paragraph 2? _____

_____

Writer's Note

The Topic Sentence

Every good paragraph has a **topic sentence**. The topic sentence tells the reader the main topic of the paragraph. Sometimes it also gives the reader a hint about the writer's purpose.

Can you find one sentence that introduces this idea? Write it here.

_____

_____

_____

10. Write the topic sentences of Paragraph 3 and Paragraph 4.

Paragraph 3: _____

_____

_____

Paragraph 4: _____

_____

_____

Supporting Sentences

The **supporting sentences** in an essay are in the body. (See pages 28–32 for information about the body.) Supporting sentences always relate to the topic sentence of the paragraph in which they occur. Common supporting sentences give examples, reasons, facts, or more specific information about the topic. Without supporting sentences, an essay would be nothing more than a general outline.

11. In Paragraph 2, the writer shows that people do not like to iron clothes. Write two of the supporting sentences here.

    _____

    _____

    _____

    _____

12. In Paragraph 4, the writer suggests that cleaning the bathroom is not a fast chore. Write the sentence in which the writer makes this point.

    _____

    _____

    _____

✎ **Writer's Note**

The Conclusion

It is important for an essay to have a good **conclusion**. Notice that the writer mentions Cinderella again in the last paragraph of "Cinderella and Her Odious Household Chores." The introduction and the conclusion often share some of the same ideas and words. (See page 33 for more information about writing the conclusion of an essay.)

13. Look at the last paragraph. Find the sentence that restates the thesis. Write that sentence here.

    _____

    _____

    _____

Building Better Sentences

Correct and varied sentence structure is essential to the quality of your writing. For further practice with "Cinderella and Her Odious Household Chores," go to Practice 1 on page 162 in Appendix 1.

ACTIVITY 2 Studying an Example Essay

Discuss the questions that come before the example essay with a partner. Then read the essay. Work with a partner to answer the questions after the essay.

In this narrative essay, the writer tells a story of a humorous language problem he experienced in Japan.

1. What are some words that cause problems for you in English? Why are they difficult?

2. Describe a situation in which you could not express yourself effectively in English. What did you do?

EXAMPLE ESSAY 2

How Do You Say . . . ?

1 What would happen if you woke up one day and suddenly found yourself in a world where you could not communicate with anyone? I am an English language teacher. In June 2004, I accepted a job in a **rural** area of Japan called Niigata and found myself faced with this language problem. One event **in particular stands out** as an example of my inability to express my ideas to the people around me **due to** my **lack** of vocabulary.

2 I had been in Japan only a few days, and I was feeling **restless**. I wanted to make some fresh bread, so I **set out for** the store with the **seemingly** simple intention of buying some flour. I had taken some Japanese language classes before I arrived in Japan. Although I knew my Japanese skills were limited, my lack of knowledge did not stop me from going to the store to buy flour. I thought that I would locate the section where the grains were displayed and find the bag that had a picture of either bread or flour on it.

3 The small town where I lived had only one tiny store. I wandered around the store a few times, but I did not see a bag of anything that appeared to be flour. In the United States, flour usually comes in a paper bag with pictures of biscuits or bread on it, so this is what I was looking for. I finally found a few clear plastic bags that had bread **crumbs** inside, so I thought that flour might be located nearby. No matter how many bags I examined, I could not find any flour.

rural: related to the countryside, the opposite of urban
in particular: especially
stand out: to be different from the other members of the group
due to: because of

a lack: a shortage
restless: impatient, agitated
set out for: to start going to a place
seemingly: apparently, supposedly
a crumb: a tiny piece of food

Example Essays   **7**

4   I desperately wanted to ask one of the three elderly women clerks where the flour was, but I could not do this simple task. I knew how to ask where something was, but I did not know the word for *flour*. I tried to think of how to say *flour* using different words, such as *white powder* or *the ingredient that you use to make bread*, but I did not know *powder* and I did not know *ingredient*. Just then, I saw one of my students in the parking lot. I rushed outside to his car and explained that I needed to know a word in Japanese. "How do you say *flour*?" I asked. He quickly replied, "That's easy." He then told me the word was *hana*.

5   I rushed back into the store, which was about to close for the evening. I found one of the elderly clerks and asked in my best Japanese, "Sumimasen. Hana-wa doko desu ka?" or "Excuse me. Where is the hana?" The petite old woman said something in Japanese and raced to the far right side of the store. Finally, I thought, "I am going to get my flour and go home to make bread." However, my hopes ended rather quickly when I followed the clerk to the **produce** section. I saw green onions, tomatoes, and even **pumpkins**, but I could not understand why flour would be there. The woman then pointed to the beautiful yellow **chrysanthemums** next to the green onions.

6   At first I was **puzzled**, but suddenly it all made sense. I had been in the country long enough to know that people in Japan eat chrysanthemums in salads. I was standing in front of the *flower* display, not the *flour* display. When I asked my student for the Japanese word for *flour*, I did not **specify** whether I meant *flour* or *flower* because it had never occurred to me that grocery stores, especially small ones, might sell flowers.

7   I did not buy any chrysanthemums that night. I was not able to find the flour, either. My lack of knowledge about Japanese cuisine and my very limited knowledge of the Japanese language caused me to go home **empty-handed** that night. However, I learned the often-underestimated value of simple vocabulary in speaking a second language. For me, this event in a small store in rural Japan opened my eyes to my lack of vocabulary skills.

produce: fresh fruits and vegetables
a pumpkin: a large, round, orange fruit
a chrysanthemum: a type of flower

puzzled: confused
specify: to say exactly
empty-handed: without getting what you hoped to get

✎ Writer's Note

Five-Paragraph Essay

The most basic and versatile format for an essay consists of five paragraphs, and you will see this format in many composition textbooks. In a typical five-paragraph essay, paragraph 1 introduces the topic, paragraphs 2–4 develop the topic by giving details, and paragraph 5 concludes the essay. An essay can range from three paragraphs to ten or more. In fact, notice how Example Essay 2 has seven paragraphs. Regardless of the length of your essay, it should always consist of an introduction, a body, and a conclusion.

3. In a few sentences, tell what happened in this story. Use your own words.

_____

_____

_____

_____

_____

_____

4. A good hook in an essay sometimes involves the reader in the information in the body of the essay. Write the hook for this essay.

_____

_____

_____

_____

5. How does this hook try to involve the reader? Do you think that this hook is successful? Why or why not?

_____

_____

_____

6. This essay tells a story. It is an organized sequence of events. This kind of essay is called a **narrative essay**. (You will learn more about narrative essays in Unit 2.) Read the list of the main events in the essay below and number the items from 1 to 12 to indicate the order in which the events took place.

_____ The clerk took the writer to the produce section.

_____ The writer asked the student for a Japanese translation.

_____ The clerk pointed to the flowers.

_____ The writer arrived in Japan.

_____ The writer wanted to make some bread.

_____ The writer spoke to an elderly clerk.

_____ The writer realized that the student had not understood the question correctly.

_____ The writer went home without the flour.

_____ The writer looked all over the store for the flour.

_____ The writer saw one of his students.

_____ The writer studied Japanese.

_____ The writer went to the store.

7. How many paragraphs are in this essay? _____ In which paragraph does the writer reveal

   what the problem is with the question he asked in Japanese? _____

8. Why does the writer include the information in Paragraph 6? (*Hint:* What supporting information
   does the writer give to explain the language miscommunication?)

   _____

   _____

Building Better Sentences

Correct and varied sentence structure is essential to the quality of your writing. Go to Practice 2 on page 163 in Appendix 1 for further practice with "How Do You Say . . . ?"

ACTIVITY 3 Studying an Example Essay

Discuss the questions that come before the example essay with a partner. Then read the essay. Work with a partner to answer the questions after the essay.

Which do you like better—the city or the countryside? Read this comparison essay about some differences between these two types of places.

1. Describe the place where you grew up.

2. What were the best and worst things about living there?

The <u>Urban</u> and Rural Divide

1   Imagine life in Tokyo. Now imagine life in a neighboring rural Japanese town. Finally, picture life in Cairo, Egypt. Which of these last two places is more different from Tokyo? Many people might mistakenly choose Cairo because it is not found in Japan. However, city **dwellers** all over the world tend to have similar lifestyles, so the biggest differences are found between Tokyo and its smaller neighbor. Urban people and rural people, **regardless of** their country, live quite differently. Perhaps some of the most **notable** differences in the lives of these two groups include the **degree** of friendliness between residents, the **pace** of life, and the variety of available activities.

2   One major difference between growing up in the city and in the country is the degree of friendliness. In large cities, residents often live in huge apartment buildings with hundreds of strangers. These urban apartment dwellers tend to be **wary** of unknown faces and rarely get to know their neighbors well. The situation in a small town is often just the opposite. Small-town people generally grow up together, attend the same schools, and share the same friends. As a result, rural people are much more likely to treat their neighbors like family and invite them into their homes.

3   Another difference is the pace of life. In the city, life moves very quickly. The streets reflect this hectic pace and are rarely empty, even late at night. City dwellers appear to be racing to get somewhere important. Life for them tends to be a series of **deadlines**. In the country, life is much slower. Even during **peak** hours, traffic jams occur less often than in a city. Stores close in the early evening, and the streets do not come alive until the next morning. The people in small towns or villages seem more relaxed and move in a more leisurely way. The pace of life in these two areas could not be more different.

4   A third difference lies in the way people are able to spend their free time. Although life in the city has its **drawbacks**, city dwellers have a much wider choice of activities that they can participate in. For example, they can go to museums, eat in exotic restaurants, attend concerts, and shop in hundreds of stores. The activities available to people in rural areas, however, are much more limited. It is rare to find museums or exotic restaurants there. Concert tours almost never include stops in country towns. Finally, people who enjoy shopping might be disappointed in the small number of stores.

5   Life in urban areas and life in rural areas vary in terms of human interaction, pace of life, and daily activities. Other important differences exist, too, but none of these makes one place better than the other. The places are simply different. Only people who have experienced living in both the city and the country can truly appreciate the unique characteristics of each.

urban: related to a city

a dweller: a person who lives in a place, resident

regardless of: in spite of

notable: important, worthy of notice

the degree: the amount

the pace: the speed, rate

wary: cautious, suspicious

the deadline: the time limit for doing something

peak: the highest, the top (amount)

a drawback: a disadvantage, a negative point

3. What is the topic of this essay?

_____

The writer's purpose is to compare and contrast life in two locations. This kind of essay is called a **comparison essay**. (You will learn more about comparison essays in Unit 3.)

4. What is the thesis statement? _____

_____

_____

5. In each paragraph, which type of location is always discussed first—rural or urban? _____

6. Which paragraph talks about activities in each area? _____ Which place offers more

   options for activities? _____

7. In Paragraph 3, the writer contrasts the pace of life in the two areas. Write the supporting sentences for the pace of life in each area.

   A. Urban

      1. _____

      2. _____

      3. _____

      4. _____

   B. Rural

      1. _____

      2. _____

      3. _____

      4. _____

Building Better Sentences

Correct and varied sentence structure is essential to the quality of your writing. For further practice with "The Urban and Rural Divide," go to Practice 3 on page 164 in Appendix 1.

Discuss the questions that come before the example essay with a partner. Then read the essay. Work with a partner to answer the questions after the essay.

This cause-effect essay tells about the connection between cancer and an unhealthy lifestyle.

1. Do you think people are healthier now than in the past? Why or why not?

2. What three changes could you make in your lifestyle to become healthier? Be specific.

EXAMPLE ESSAY 4

Cancer Risks

1   Lung cancer kills more people in one year than all criminal and accidental deaths combined. This statistic is shocking, but the good news is that people are now well-informed about the risks connected to lung cancer. They know that their risk of contracting this terrible disease decreases if they either stop smoking or do not smoke at all. Unfortunately, the same cannot be said about other types of cancer. Many people are not aware that their everyday behavior can lead to the development of different forms of cancer. By eating better, exercising regularly, and staying out of the sun, people can reduce their risks of cancer.

2   Instead of foods that are good for them, people often eat unhealthy foods, such as hamburgers, french fries, and pizza. These popular foods contain large amounts of saturated fat, which is one of the worst kinds of fat. Although light and fat-free products are constantly being introduced to the consumer market, many people still buy foods that contain fat because they often taste better. However, eating fatty foods can increase a person's chances for some kinds of cancer. People do not eat as many fresh vegetables and fresh fruits as they used to. Instead, they now eat a lot more processed foods that do not contain natural **fiber**. Lack of fiber in a person's diet can increase the chance of **colon** cancer. In the past, people with less information about nutrition actually had better **diets** than people do today. They also had fewer cases of cancer.

3   Many people today are overweight, and being overweight has been connected to some kinds of cancer. Since television sets are now a standard piece of furniture in most living rooms, people spend more time sitting down and mindlessly eating snacks than they did in the past. The first generation of TV watchers started the **couch potato boom**, and today's couch potatoes are bigger than ever. Health experts warn that being overweight is a risk not only for heart disease but also

fiber: a plant material that is good for the digestive system

colon: an organ in the digestive system

diet: what a person eats, a special plan for losing weight

a couch potato: a person who spends a lot of time on the couch, usually watching TV

a boom: a sudden increase in popularity

for certain kinds of cancer. The best way to **attain** a healthy weight is for people to **cut back on** the amount of food that they consume and to exercise regularly. It is not possible to do only one of these and lose weight permanently. The improved diet must be **in conjunction with** regular exercise. In the past, people did more physical activity than people do today. For example, people used to walk to work; now almost no one does. In addition, people had jobs that required more physical labor. Now many people have desk jobs in front of computers.

4   Finally, health officials are gravely concerned by the **astounding** rise in the cases of skin cancer. Many societies value a tanned complexion, so on weekends people tend to **flock to** the beach or swimming pools and lie in the sun. Many of these people do not use a safe sunscreen, and the result is that they often get sunburned. Sunburn damages the skin, and repeated damage may lead to skin cancer later in life. Once the damage is done, it cannot be undone. Thus, prevention is important. In the past, people did not lie in direct sunlight for long periods of time, and skin cancer was not as **prevalent** as it is now. People have started to listen to doctors' warnings about this situation, and more and more people are using proper sunscreens. Unfortunately, millions of people already have this potential cancer problem in their skin and may develop cancer later.

5   Cancer has been around since the earliest days of human existence, but only recently has the public been made aware of some of the risk factors involved. Antismoking campaigns can be seen everywhere—on billboards, in television commercials, on the radio, and in newsprint. If the same amount of attention were given to proper diets, exercise, and sunscreens, perhaps the number of overall cancer cases could be reduced.

attain: to achieve
cut back on: to reduce the amount (of something)
in conjunction with: at the same time as, together with

astounding: amazing, surprising
flock to: to go to a place in large numbers (as birds do)
prevalent: common

3. What is the writer's main message in this essay? _____

_____

_____

The writer presents several causes for the rise in the number of cancer cases. This kind of organization is called a **cause-effect essay**. (You will learn more about cause-effect essays in Unit 4.) In this kind of essay, the writer shows that one thing happened (effect) because something else happened first (cause).

4. What is the thesis statement of this essay?

_____

_____

5. The thesis statement should tell the reader how the essay will be organized. What do you know about the organization of the essay from the thesis statement?

_____

_____

6. In Paragraph 2, the writer states that many people eat unhealthy food. What supporting information explains why this food is not healthy?

_____

_____

_____

7. In Paragraph 2, the writer also explains why people enjoy eating unhealthy foods. Write the reason here.

_____

🔨 Building Better Sentences

Correct and varied sentence structure is essential to the quality of your writing. For further practice with "Cancer Risks," go to Practice 4 on page 165 in Appendix 1.

ACTIVITY 5 Studying an Example Essay

Discuss the questions that come before the example essay with a partner. Then read the essay. Work with a partner to answer the questions after the essay.

Choosing a college is an important decision. This essay may help you decide what type of college to attend.

1. What do you know about community colleges? How are they different from universities?

2. What are some things that students consider when they are choosing a college?

EXAMPLE ESSAY 5

An Alternative to University Education

1   A high school diploma is not the end of many people's education these days. High school students who want to continue their education generally choose one of two routes after graduation. Some students **opt to** attend a community college and then transfer to a university while others go directly to a university. Making this difficult choice requires a great deal of careful thought. However, if the choice is based on three specific factors, **namely**, cost, location, and quality of education, students will quickly see the advantages that attending a community college offers.

2   Attending a community college is much cheaper than attending a university. For example, **tuition** at a local community college might cost $2,000 per year, especially for residents of the area. The same classes taken at a nearby university would cost almost $5,000. In addition, a university would charge more for parking, photocopying at the library, cafeteria food, campus health clinic services, and textbooks. No matter how the total bill is calculated or what is included, it is more expensive to study at a university.

3   Studying at a community college can be more convenient because of its location. Going to a university often requires recent high school graduates to live far from home, and many of them are **reluctant** to do so. These students are only seventeen or eighteen years old and may have very little experience with being away from home. It is often difficult for these young people to suddenly find themselves far away from their families. In addition, very few parents are prepared to send their teenagers to distant universities. Because almost every area has a community college, students who opt to go to a community college first can continue to be near their families for two more years.

4   Finally, there are educational benefits to attending a community college. University life is very different from community college life. A university campus offers a large variety of sports events and social activities, and students can easily become distracted from their studies. Community colleges, which typically have fewer students and extracurricular activities, may be a better environment for serious study. In addition, the library facilities at a community college, though not as large as those at a university, are more than sufficient for the kind of work that is required in first- or second-year courses. Class size is also an issue to consider. Introductory courses at universities often have 50, 60, or even 100 students. In such large classes, student-teacher interaction is **minimal**, and learning can be more difficult for some students. Finally, the teaching at community colleges is often better than the teaching at a university. Professors at community colleges have the same **credentials** as those at universities, but community college professors spend most of their time teaching instead of conducting research, as university professors have to do.

5   The decision to enter a university directly or to attend a community college for the first two years after high school can be difficult. Community colleges are not as glamorous as large universities. They are often seen as second-rate alternatives to the more well-known universities. However, based on the three important factors outlined above—cost, location, and quality of education—it is clear that for many students, choosing a community college is the smarter thing to do.

opt to: to choose to (do something)   **reluctant:** hesitant
namely: such as, for example, that is   **minimal:** the least amount possible
tuition: money paid for classes   **credentials:** qualifications

3. What two things are being compared in this essay?

_____

Which one does the writer think is better?

_____

In essays like this one, the writer is comparing two or more things. However, unlike the writer of "The Urban and Rural Divide" (Example Essay 3, page 11), the writer of "An Alternative to University Education" compares community colleges and universities with the intention of persuading the reader that community colleges are often better for new high school graduates. This kind of essay is called an **argumentative essay**. (You will learn more about argumentative essays in Unit 5.) Some books call this type of essay a persuasive essay.

4. What is the organization of this essay? Fill in the blanks of this simple outline with the words that are missing.

Topic: The Advantages of Community Colleges

I. Introduction (Paragraph 1)

Thesis statement: _____

_____

II. Body

  A. Paragraph 2 topic: _____

    1. Tuition

      a. Community college: $ _____

      b. _____ : $ _____

    2. Other costs

      a. Parking

      b. _____

      c. _____

      d. Health clinic services

      e. _____

SUPPORT

B. Paragraph 3 topic: Location

    1. Better for students

       a. _____

       b. _____

    2. Better for parents

C. Paragraph 4 topic: _____

    1. Distractions of university

    2. Community college: Quiet campus

    3. _____

    4. Class size

    5. Quality of teaching

III. Conclusion (Paragraph 5)

5. The writer discusses three factors—cost, location, and quality of education—in the decision about what kind of college to attend. Can you think of two other factors that the writer could have used?

_____

_____

6. Before you read this essay, did you know much about this topic? What was your opinion before you read this essay? (Check all possible answers.)

_____ I thought that attending a university directly after high school was better.

_____ I thought that attending a community college after high school was better.

_____ I thought that a university offered a better education than a community college.

_____ I thought that a community college offered a better education than a university.

_____ I thought that a university was cheaper than a community college.

_____ I thought that a community college was cheaper than a university.

_____ I did not know much about university education.

_____ I did not know much about community college education.

7. Did your opinion about community colleges change after you read "An Alternative to University Education"? In other words, did the writer persuade you to change your mind about community colleges?

_____

_____

8. Which part of the essay was the most persuasive for you?

_____

_____

9. If your answer to Item 7 is *yes*, tell why your opinion changed. If your answer to Item 7 is *no*, write three specific reasons why you still believe a university is a better choice.

_____

_____

_____

_____

Building Better Sentences

Correct and varied sentence structure is essential to the quality of your writing. For further practice with "An Alternative to University Education," go to Practice 5 on page 166 in Appendix 1.

Writing the Introduction

The **introduction** is the first part of an essay, usually the first paragraph. The introduction does not have to be written first however. Some writers design and write this part of the essay last or at another point in their writing process.

From the basic outline that follows, you can see how the introduction fits into the essay.

    I. Introduction (usually one paragraph)
   II. Body (one to four paragraphs)
 III. Conclusion (usually one paragraph)

There are many ways to write an introduction. Some writers begin with a question. Other writers give background information about the topic. The kind of introduction you choose depends on how you want to present the topic and the kind of essay you decide to write.

What Is in the Introduction?

The introduction for most essays is one paragraph. This introductory paragraph usually consists of three parts:

$$\text{INTRODUCTION} = \begin{cases} 1. \text{ The hook} \\ 2. \text{ Connecting information} \\ 3. \text{ The thesis statement (or writing plan)} \end{cases}$$

Now look at each of these parts to see what they are and how they work in the introduction.

The **hook** is the opening statement or statements of an essay. Just as people use a hook at the end of a fishing pole to catch a fish, writers use a hook to catch the readers' attention. If a hook does its job well, readers will want to read the rest of the essay after they have read the hook. Writing a good hook is not easy. It requires a great deal of thought and practice.

There are many different ways to write a hook.

1. **Ask a question.** If readers want to know the answer to the question, they are "hooked" and will read the essay. For example, a writer might begin an essay about the need for more government regulation of medicine with this question:

    How many people take medicine—even simple aspirin—every day?

    Most readers will not know the answer to this question, but they will probably be interested and want to find out more about the topic.

2. **Use an interesting observation.** Here is an example:

    Asian economists are not sleeping well these days.

    This observation makes readers want to know why economists are not sleeping well. This hook leads to the main idea of the essay, which will highlight the three main causes of recession in Asia.

    Here is another example of an observation hook full of interesting details that leads readers to the topic of international trade:

    The average Canadian is proud to be Canadian and can easily talk about the benefits of living in Canada. However, many Canadians drive Japanese or German cars to work every morning. They wear cotton shirts made in Honduras and pants made in Bangladesh. Their dinner salad may contain tomatoes from California and salad dressing from France. Before going to bed, Canadians will most likely watch their favorite TV programs on a Japanese or Korean television.

3. **Use a unique scenario to catch readers' attention.** Here is an example:

    Traveling at more than one hundred miles an hour, he feels as though he is not moving. He is engulfed in complete silence. For a moment, it is as if he has entered another dimension.

    Are you hooked? Do you want to read the rest of the essay? This essay is about the exciting sport of skydiving.

4. **Begin with a famous quote.** Study this example:

    "I have a dream."

    Many readers may think that this hook will lead into a discussion of Martin Luther King, Jr.'s life or his struggles. In fact, this hook begins an essay on the topic of sleep patterns.

5. **Use a surprising or shocking statistic.** Here are two examples:

Over 20,000 people in the United States are killed in alcohol-related traffic accidents every year.

If world temperatures continue to rise, Singapore and New York may be under water by the year 2050.

 For practice with identifying the hook, try Unit 1, Activity 2 on the *Great Writing 4* Web site: elt.heinle.com/greatwriting

Writer's Note

Hook versus Main Idea

In English writing, the main idea, or thesis, of an essay is usually in the introduction, but it is not often the first sentence. (The hook is usually the first sentence or the first few sentences.) You can begin an essay with a sentence stating the main idea:

This essay will talk about the most embarrassing day of my life.

or

There are three ways to curb your appetite.

However, in academic writing, beginning with a sentence that plainly states the main idea is <u>not</u> preferred. Because it gives away the main idea of the essay too soon, your readers may not be interested in reading the rest of your essay. Stating the main idea will not grab your readers' attention, so be sure to begin your essay with an interesting hook.

 For practice with the hook versus the main idea, try Unit 1, Activity 3 on the *Great Writing 4* Web site: elt.heinle.com/greatwriting

Connecting Information

After the hook, the writer usually writes **connecting information**, or three to five sentences that help connect the reader to the topic. These sentences can be background information about the topic or they can be examples. The following sentences from Example Essay 1 on pages 3–4 give examples of how Cinderella probably spent her days before she met the prince:

Her daily routine was not glamorous. She did everything from sweeping the floors to cooking the meals. If someone had asked Cinderella which chores she did not particularly like, she probably would have answered, "Why, none, of course. Housework is my duty!"

From these sentences, the reader has a good idea of what the topic might be—unpleasant household chores.

What Does the Reader Know?

A good writer does not jump into a topic too quickly. First, a good writer tries to imagine what the reader already knows about the topic. Then the writer can focus on bridging the gap between what the reader knows and what he or she needs to know about the topic. It is very important to keep the reader (the audience) in mind when writing academic essays.

The Thesis Statement

The **thesis statement**, or writing plan, is usually the last part of the introduction. It can be one or two sentences long. In the thesis statement, the writer tells the reader what to expect in the essay. Basically, there are two kinds of thesis statements—**stated** and **implied**. (They may also be called direct and indirect thesis statements.)

Stated Thesis Statement Some writers want to give a specific outline of their essays in their thesis statements. Read the following example:

> *The main problems facing South American countries are a lack of job opportunities for citizens, increasing demand for better health care, and limited university programs for poor students.*

From this statement, the reader knows that the body of the essay has three main parts. The first part will discuss job opportunities, the second part will talk about health-care needs, and the last part will talk about university programs for poor students. This kind of thesis statement is called a stated thesis.

Implied Thesis Statement Other writers are not so direct. Discussing a similar topic as the previous example, these writers might use this statement:

> *The important problems facing South American countries today require immediate attention.*

From this statement, the reader expects to find a discussion of problems in South America. The reader is not given the specific information that will follow in the essay, but the general topic is clear. In this case, the reader must continue reading to find the supporting ideas of the argument. This kind of thesis statement is called an implied thesis.

Both stated and implied thesis statements are acceptable. It is up to the writer or the instructor to decide which approach to take.

 For practice with identifying the type of thesis statement, try Unit 1, Activity 4 on the *Great Writing 4* Web site: elt.heinle.com/greatwriting

Practice with Hooks and Thesis Statements

The following activities will give you practice writing hooks. You will also compare your hooks with hooks written by your classmates. This will help you improve your understanding of how hooks work in essay introductions. Be prepared to explain why you think your hook will attract readers' attention and make them want to read the essay. You will also practice writing and identifying thesis statements.

ACTIVITY 6 Practice with Hooks

In this argumentative essay, the writer argues that mandatory retirement should be abolished. The essay begins with the connecting information. First, read the entire essay. Then go back and write three possible hooks that would capture the readers' attention.

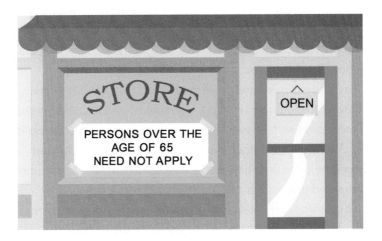

EXAMPLE ESSAY 6

No More Mandatory Retirement

1   Hook 1: _____

_____

_____

_____

Hook 2: _____

_____

_____

_____

Hook 3: _____

_____

_____

_____

Traditionally, people retire from their jobs when they reach the age of 65. In some jobs, this is not an option but a requirement. Mandatory retirement for capable workers is wrong because it violates personal choice, discriminates against senior citizens, and wastes valuable skills as well as money.

2   One reason that mandatory retirement is wrong is that it takes away an individual's personal choice of either continuing to work or retiring. The older working person should have the right to choose his or her retirement age. A person's right to life, liberty, and the pursuit of happiness (as written in the Declaration of Independence) is a very special thing. Forced retirement takes away people's livelihood, deprives them of their freedom to choose how to spend their time, and prevents them from pursuing happiness.

3   Second, mandatory retirement is surely a form of age discrimination. A young person might wonder why an older worker should be kept on the payroll when the company could hire someone who is younger and more creative. However, a younger person would not necessarily be a better or more creative worker. Age does not indicate the quality of a person's work. Many well-known artists, politicians, and writers developed their best works after the age of 60. The common belief that a person's mind slows down after a certain age is nothing but a misconception.

4   In addition to the previous two points, quality of work is another important issue. Older employees have knowledge and experience that can truly be beneficial to a company. Unfortunately, many employers disregard this fact. Captain Al Haynes, aged 58, was able to land a DC-10 that was out of control so that 186 of the 296 people aboard survived when it crashed. The aircraft manufacturer simulated the same situation 45 times, and not one time did they have a successful landing. Safety experts agree that the high survival rate among the passengers on the flight was due to Captain Haynes's aviation skills. It is doubtful that a less experienced pilot could have accomplished this feat. However, two years later, Captain Haynes had to retire because he had reached the age of 60, the mandatory retirement age for pilots in the United States.

5   Many people, especially fresh college graduates, do not agree that retirement should be an option. They are worried that if older workers are allowed to continue in their jobs, there will not be enough openings for younger people. However, is there really a danger that older people will take away job opportunities from younger people? This situation is unlikely because younger workers and older workers rarely compete for the same jobs. The reality is that older workers rarely seek entry-level positions. Therefore, employers should start looking for ways to attract experienced workers, not retire them.

6   In conclusion, the age of retirement should be decided by an individual's economic need, health status, and personal preference. People's lives are their own, and they should be allowed to live them to their fullest potential. Without a doubt, mandatory retirement goes against fulfilling this potential and should not be a part of modern society.

In pairs or small groups, share the three hooks that you wrote with your classmates. Are any of them similar? Explain why you think your hooks will grab readers' attention.

ACTIVITY 7 Thesis Statement Questions

Answer these questions about the thesis statement in "No More Mandatory Retirement."

1. What is the thesis statement in the essay?

   _____

   _____

2. Is this a stated or implied thesis statement? _____ Give the reason for your answer.

   _____

   _____

3. Rewrite the thesis statement using the alternative form. _____

   _____

   _____

   _____

🔨 Building Better Sentences

Correct and varied sentence structure is essential to the quality of your writing. For further practice with "No More Mandatory Retirement," go to Practice 6 on page 167 in Appendix 1.

ACTIVITY 8 More Practice with Hooks

This comparison essay compares two different types of jobs. The essay begins with the connecting information. First, read the whole essay. Then go back and write three possible hooks that would capture the readers' attention.

The Truth about Coaches and Business Managers

1   Hook 1: _____

_____

_____

_____

Hook 2: _____

_____

_____

_____

Hook 3: _____

_____

_____

_____

Coaches work outdoors while business managers stay in offices. Coaches train athletes' bodies, but managers are more focused on detail-oriented matters. These differences, however, pale in comparison to the similarities shared by the two professions, for the main functions of athletic team coaches and business managers are very closely related.

2   One of the most fundamental similarities between athletic team coaches and business managers is the task of leading the team members or employees. Coaches are responsible for training their athletes and focusing on each individual's strengths and weaknesses. Coaches also give directions to their players to improve their performance and commonly give feedback after a game. Similarly, business managers are responsible for the proper training of their employees. Managers use their people skills to ensure that each worker is put in the job that suits his or her abilities best. In addition, managers typically give periodic reviews of their employees as feedback on their job performance.

3   Another important similarity between the two professions is the ability to solve problems between teammates or employees. Athletes tend to be very competitive, and often this competitiveness leads to arguments in practice and during games. Coaches know that this behavior is not productive in leading the team to victory, so they often act as intermediaries. They listen to both sides and usually come up with words of wisdom or advice to straighten out the problem. In the same way, a manager is often asked to mediate between two or more employees who might not be getting along in the office. Managers know that teamwork is vital to productivity, so they are trained to make sure that the workplace runs smoothly.

4 Finally, both coaches and managers must represent their subordinates to the members of higher management. Many social groups function as hierarchies, and the locker room and office are no different. Coaches are regularly asked to report to the team owners with updates on the season. They write up reports to keep the owners informed about who is doing well, who is injured, and who is not performing up to par. In addition, they serve as the players' spokespersons. If players have a particular problem related to something other than their athletic performance, it is usually the coaches who end up speaking with the owners on the players' behalf. Like coaches, business managers are the links between the CEOs and lower-level employees. The business managers are given the tasks of overseeing employees and serving as go-betweens. Top management wants to remain aware of what is happening in the company, but they usually do not have the time to deal with such details. Business managers, therefore, serve as spokespeople to both ends of the hierarchy.

5 On the surface, the two occupations seem completely unrelated. The coach works outdoors and handles the pressures of physical exercise and game strategies while the business manager works in a formal environment surrounded by modern technology. Upon further inspection, however, these two occupations are very closely related. Both coaches and managers are the glue that holds the members of the team together.

In pairs or small groups, share the three hooks that you wrote with your classmates. Are any of them similar? Explain why you think your hooks will attract readers' attention.

ACTIVITY 9 Thesis Statement Questions

Answer these questions about the thesis statement in "The Truth about Coaches and Business Managers."

1. What is the thesis statement in the essay?

   _____

   _____

   _____

2. Is this a stated or implied thesis? _____ Give the reason for your answer.

   _____

   _____

3. Rewrite the thesis statement using the alternative form.

   _____

   _____

   _____

Building Better Sentences

Correct and varied sentence structure is essential to the quality of your writing. For further practice with "The Truth about Coaches and Business Managers," go to Practice 7 on page 168 in Appendix 1.

Writing the Body

The **body** of an essay is the essay's main part. It usually consists of three or four paragraphs between the introduction and the conclusion. The body follows a plan of organization that the writer usually determines before he or she starts writing. This organization varies depending on the kind of essay you are writing.

You can write the organizational plan of your essay in an **outline**. There are different levels of outlining. A **general outline** includes the main points, while a **specific**, or **detailed**, **outline** includes notes on even the smallest pieces of information that will go into the essay. It is much easier to write an essay from a specific outline than from a general outline. However, most writers start with a general outline first and then add details.

Writer's Note

Using an Outline

The best essays have well-planned outlines that are prepared before the writer starts writing. By spending more time in this pre-writing stage, the writer can organize his or her thoughts, often moving them around until the information looks cohesive in the outline. Once it is time to write the essay, the organization and flow of ideas will have already been reviewed.

Here is a general outline and a specific outline for Example Essay 7, "The Truth about Coaches and Business Managers," pages 26–27. Read and compare the two outlines.

General Outline	Specific Outline
I. Introduction	I. Introduction
A. Hook: Pose a question	A. Hook: Are athletic coaches similar to business managers?
B. Connecting information	B. Connecting information: They work in different places and focus on different jobs.
C. Thesis: Similarities in coaches' and managers' jobs	C. Thesis: The two professions share many similarities, for the main functions of athletic team coaches and business managers are very closely related.

II. Body

    A. Similarity 1: Leading the athletes and employees

    B. Similarity 2: Solving problems

    C. Similarity 3: Representing the athletes and employees

III. Conclusion
    Focus on maintaining communication

II. Body

    A. Similarity 1: Leading the athletes and employees

        1. Coaches train athletes

            a. Focus on strengths

            b. Focus on weaknesses

            c. Give feedback

        2. Managers train employees

            a. Put employees in jobs that fit them best

            b. Perform job reviews

    B. Similarity 2: Solving problems

        1. Coaches listen to athletes

            a. Stop fights

            b. Act as go-betweens

        2. Managers mediate in office

            a. Stress importance of teamwork with employees

            b. Try to get officemates to cooperate

    C. Similarity 3: Representing the athletes and employees

        1. Coaches to owners

            a. Give updates to owners

            b. Discuss athletes' problems

        2. Managers to CEOs

            a. Maintain control on behalf of the bosses

            b. Update the CEOs on employee issues

III. Conclusion: Both careers are fundamental in improving communication and keeping the team together.

Practice with Outlining an Essay

General Outline

ACTIVITY 10 Making a General Outline

Here is a general outline for Example Essay 2, "How Do You Say . . . ?," on pages 7–8. Read the essay again and complete this outline.

Title: _____

  I. Introduction (Paragraph 1)

     A. Hook: Ask a general question

     B. Connecting information

     C. Thesis statement: _____

             _____

  II. Body

     A. Paragraph 2 topic sentence: _____

             _____

     B. Paragraph 3 topic sentence: _____

             _____

     C. Paragraph 4 topic sentence: _____

             _____

     D. Paragraph 5 topic sentence: _____

             _____

     E. Paragraph 6 topic sentence: At first I was puzzled, but suddenly it all made sense.

  III. Conclusion (Paragraph 7)

     A. End of action

     B. Restatement of thesis

ACTIVITY 11 Making a Specific Outline

Here is a specific outline for Example Essay 1, "Cinderella and Her Odious Household Chores," on pages 3–4. Read the essay again and complete this outline. You may use complete sentences if you wish, but be sure to include all of the specific information.

Title: _____

I. Introduction (Paragraph 1)

  A. Hook: _____

    _____

  B. Connecting information: _____

    _____

    _____

  C. Thesis statement: _____

    _____

II. Body

  A. Paragraph 2

    1. Topic sentence (Chore #1): _____

      _____

    2. Supporting ideas

      a. Attention to detail

        (1) Smoothing out the fabric

        (2) Following the seams

        (3) _____

        (4) _____

      b. Problem: _____

      _____

SUPPORT

B. Paragraph 3

    1. Topic sentence (Chore #2): _____

    _____

    2. Supporting ideas

SUPPORT

        a. Why we cannot depend on dishwashers

        b. Negative aspects of this chore

            (1) Elbow grease

            (2) _____

            (3) _____

C. Paragraph 4

    1. Topic sentence (Chore #3): _____

    _____

    2. Supporting ideas

        a. Tasks

            (1) _____

            (2) Cleaning the sink

            (3) Cleaning the toilet

SUPPORT

        b. Negative aspects

            (1) Bathroom is full of germs

            (2) _____

        c. Positive aspect: _____

III. Conclusion (Paragraph 5)

    A. Maintaining a house includes chores.

    B. People get through the three odious chores by taking pride in doing a good job.

Writer's Note

Outline Length

    If your outline is too long, combine some of the ideas or eliminate ideas that do not add interest to the essay.

Writing the Conclusion

Some people think that writing the conclusion is the hardest part of writing an essay. For others, writing the conclusion is easy. When you write a conclusion, follow these guidelines:

1. Let the reader know that this is the conclusion. You can mark the conclusion with some kind of transition or connector that tells the reader that this is the final paragraph of the essay. (See the *Brief Writer's Handbook with Activities*, pages 156–157, for a list of connectors.) Here are some examples:

    In conclusion,   *From the information given,*   *To summarize,*

    Sometimes the first sentence of the conclusion restates the thesis or main idea of the essay:

    As previously noted, there are numerous problems that new parents face today.

2. Do not introduce new information in the conclusion. The conclusion should help the reader to reconsider the main ideas that you have given in the essay. Any new information in the concluding paragraph will sound like a continuation of the body of the essay.

3. Many writers find the conclusion difficult to write. It requires a great deal of thought and creativity, just as writing a good hook or thesis statement does. The kind of essay you are writing may determine the way you end the essay; however, the following ideas can be helpful for any essay.

    a. The final sentence or sentences of an essay often give a suggestion, an opinion, or a prediction about the topic of the essay.

        -   **Suggestion:** *In order for young people to successfully learn a language, parents need to encourage them at an early age.*

        -   **Opinion:** *Learning a second language at an early age is, in effect, a smart choice.*

        -   **Prediction:** *If more young people were bilingual, perhaps they would better understand the complex world around them.*

    b. Sometimes the final sentence or sentences simply say that the issue has been discussed in the essay with so many strong, persuasive facts that the answer to the issue is now clear.

        Once aware of this information, any reader would agree that bilingual education is an excellent educational opportunity.

 For practice with identifying types of concluding sentences, try Unit 1, Activity 5 on the *Great Writing 4* Web site: elt.heinle.com/greatwriting

✎ Writer's Note

Checking the First and Last Paragraphs

After you write your essay, read the introductory paragraph and the concluding paragraph. These two paragraphs should contain similar information.

 For practice with checking the first and last paragraphs, try Unit 1, Activity 6 on the *Great Writing 4* Web site: elt.heinle.com/greatwriting

ACTIVITY 12 Word Associations

Circle the word or phrase that is most closely related to the word or phrase on the left. If necessary, use a dictionary to check the meaning of words you do not know. The first one has been done for you.

1. a chore	pleasant	(unpleasant)
2. a lack	enough	not enough
3. the produce	food items	purchased items
4. rural	many people	few people
5. wary	confident	suspicious
6. tuition	money	work
7. reluctant	repetitive	hesitant
8. a drawback	negative	positive
9. a routine	surprising	habit
10. prevalent	common	rare

ACTIVITY 13 Using Collocations

Fill in each blank with the word on the left that most naturally completes the phrase on the right. If necessary, use a dictionary to check the meaning of words you do not know. The first one has been done for you.

1. computer / basis   on a daily _____ basis _____

2. has / makes   it _____ sense

3. by / with   in conjunction _____

4. claim / entail   some people _____ that

5. with / as   the same credentials _____

6. detergent / grease   elbow _____

7. of / against   to discriminate _____

8. glamorous / management   higher _____

9. fat / wide   a _____ variety of

10. tackle / wrinkle   to _____ a difficult task

Original Student Writing

Writer's Note

Understanding the Writing Process: The Seven Steps

There are many ways to write, but most good writers follow certain steps in the writing process.

Step 1: **Choose a topic.** Ideally, the topic should be something that interests you.

Step 2: **Brainstorm.** Write down as many ideas as you can about your chosen topic; you will move things around and change ideas as you reach Step 3.

Step 3: **Outline.** Once you have a topic and a thesis statement, it is time to put your ideas into a logical format. Write an outline to help you organize how you will present your ideas.

Step 4: **Write the first draft.** Use the information from your brainstorming session and your outline to write a first draft. At this stage, do not worry about errors in your writing. Focus on putting your ideas into sentences.

Step 5: **Get feedback from a peer.** The more feedback you have, the better. Your classmates can help you with the content and organization of your paper, as can your instructor.

Step 6: **Revise the first draft.** Based on the feedback you receive, consider making some changes.

Step 7: **Proofread the final draft.** Review the final paper before you turn it in. Be sure it is typed, double-spaced, and free of any grammatical and spelling errors.

For more detailed information on the seven steps of the writing process, see the Brief Writer's Handbook with Activities, pages 131–138.

ACTIVITY 14 Essay Writing Practice

Write an essay on one of the following suggested topics. Depending on the topic that you choose, you may need to do some research. Use at least five of the vocabulary words or phrases presented in Activity 12 and Activity 13. Underline these words and phrases in your essay. Before you write, be sure to refer to the seven steps in the writing process in the Writer's Note above.

Additional Topics for Writing

TOPIC 1: Write an essay about an important event that changed your life, such as marriage, the birth of a child, moving to a foreign country, or the loss of someone close to you.

TOPIC 2: Describe a festival or celebration in your culture. Discuss the history of the event, its meaning, and how it is celebrated.

TOPIC 3: Many inventions of the twentieth century, such as the cell phone or laptop computer, have changed our lives. Write an essay in which you discuss the effects of one recent invention on society.

TOPIC 4: Some people say that individuals are born with their intelligence and that outside factors do not affect intelligence very much. They believe that nature (what we are born with) is more important than nurture (environment). Other people say that intelligence is mainly the result of the interaction between people and their environment. These people believe that nurture is more important than nature. Write an essay in which you defend one of these points of view.

TOPIC 5: Write about a movie that you saw recently. Begin by summarizing the story; then tell what you liked and did not like about it.

Timed Writing

How quickly can you write in English? There are many times when you must write quickly, such as on a test. It is important to feel comfortable during those times. Timed-writing practice can make you feel better about writing quickly in English.

First, read the essay guidelines below. Then take out a piece of paper. Read the writing prompt below the guidelines. As quickly as you can, brainstorm some ideas about this essay topic. You should spend <u>no more than</u> 5 minutes on brainstorming.

You will then have 40 minutes to write a basic 5-paragraph essay about your topic. At the end of the 40 minutes, your teacher will collect your work and return it to you at a later date.

Essay Guidelines

- Remember to give your essay a title.

- Double-space your essay.

- Write as legibly as possible (if you are not using a computer).

- Include a short introduction (with a thesis statement), three body paragraphs, and a conclusion.

- Try to give yourself a few minutes before the end of the activity to review your work. Check for spelling, verb tense, and subject-verb agreement mistakes.

> What are the benefits of knowing a second language?

Narrative Essays

GOAL: To learn how to write a narrative essay

*Language Focus: Connectors and time relationship words

What Is a Narrative Essay?

A **narrative essay** tells a story. Telling stories has always been an important part of human history. Another word for *story* is *narrative*. Even though the narrative essay has the same basic form as most other academic essays, it allows the writer to be more creative than academic essays usually do.

Several important elements make up a story:

Setting	The setting is the location where the action in a story takes place.
Theme	The theme is the basic idea of the story. Very often the theme will deal with a topic that is common in life or human nature, such as greed, envy, love, independence, and courage.
Mood	The mood is the feeling or atmosphere that the writer creates for the story. It could be happy, hopeful, suspenseful, or scary. Both the setting and descriptive vocabulary create the mood in a narrative.
Characters	The characters are the people in the story. They are affected by the mood of the story, and they react to the events in which they are involved.
Plot	The plot is what happens in the story, that is, the sequence of events. The plot often includes a climax or turning point at which the characters or events change.

 For practice with identifying the elements of a story, try Unit 2, Activity 1 on the *Great Writing 4* Web site: elt.heinle.com/greatwriting

The Introduction

The **introduction** of a narrative essay is the paragraph that begins your story. In the introduction, you describe the setting, introduce the characters, and prepare your audience for the action to come. Of course, the introduction should have a hook and a thesis.

The Narrative Hook

You learned in Unit 1 that the **hook** in an essay is the part of the introduction—usually the first few sentences—that grabs readers' attention. Hooks are especially important in narrative essays because they help set the stage for the story. The hook makes readers start guessing about what will happen next. Let's look at the hook from Example Essay 8 that you will read in Activity 2.

> *I had never been more anxious in my life. I had just spent the last three endless hours trying to get to the airport so that I could travel home.*

Does this hook make you want to know what happened to the narrator? The hook should make the reader ask *wh-* questions about the essay. You may have thought of questions like these when you read the preceding hook:

- <u>Who</u> is the narrator and why is he or she anxious?
- <u>Where</u> is the airport?
- <u>What</u> made the trip to the airport seem endless?
- <u>Why</u> is this person going home?

ACTIVITY 1 Identifying Hooks

Read the sentences below. Which three sentences would <u>not</u> be good hooks for a narrative essay? Put an X next to these sentences. Be ready to explain why you think these sentences do not work well as hooks for narrative essays.

1. _____ The roar of race-car engines ripped through the blazing heat of the day.

2. _____ It was freezing on that sad December day.

3. _____ After my brother's accident, I sat alone in the hospital waiting room.

4. _____ My friend and I should not have been walking home alone so late on that dark winter night.

5. _____ Whales are by far the largest marine mammals.

6. _____ She gave her friend a birthday gift.

7. _____ The gleaming snow lay over the treacherous mountain like a soft white blanket, making the terrain seem safe instead of deadly.

8. _____ The Russian dictionary that we use in our language class has 500 pages.

9. _____ Amber never expected to hear the deadly sound of a rattlesnake in her kitchen garden.

10. _____ A shot rang out in the silence of the night.

For more practice with identifying hooks, try Unit 2, Activity 2 on the *Great Writing 4* Web site: elt.heinle.com/greatwriting

The Thesis

In most types of essays, the **thesis** states the main idea of the essay and tells what the organization of the information will be. However, in a narrative essay, the thesis introduces the action that begins in the first paragraph of the essay. Look at these example thesis statements:

- *Now, as I watched the bus driver set my luggage on the airport sidewalk, I realized that my frustration had only just begun.*

- *I wanted my mother to watch me race down the steep hill, so I called out her name and then nudged my bike forward.*

- *Because his pride would not allow him to apologize, Ken now had to fight the bully, and he was pretty sure that he would not win.*

These thesis statements do not tell the reader what happens. They only introduce the action that will follow. The paragraphs in the body will develop the story.

The Body

The **body** of your narrative essay contains most of the plot—the supporting information. The action in the plot can be organized in many different ways. One way is **chronological**, or time, order. In this method, each paragraph gives more information about the story as it proceeds in time—the first paragraph usually describes the first event, the second paragraph describes the second event, and so on.

Transitional Sentences

In an essay with chronological organization, each paragraph ends with a **transitional sentence**. Transitional sentences have two purposes: (1) to signal the end of the action in one paragraph and (2) to provide a link to the action of the next paragraph. These sentences are vital because they give your story unity and allow the reader to follow the action easily. The following example is from Example Essay 8 on page 41, Paragraphs 2 and 3. Notice how the ideas in the last sentence of Paragraph 2 (the transitional sentence, underlined) and the first sentence of Paragraph 3 (italicized) are connected.

2   This was my first visit to the international section of the airport, and nothing was familiar. I could not make sense of all the signs. Where was the ticket counter? Where should I take my luggage? I had no idea where the customs line was. I began to panic. What time was it? Where was my airplane? <u>I had to find help because I could not be late!</u>

3   *I tried to ask a passing businessman for help, but all my words came out wrong.* He just scowled and walked away. What had happened? I had been in this country for a whole semester, and I could not even remember how to ask for directions. This was awful! Another bus arrived at the terminal, and the passengers came out carrying all sorts of luggage. Here was my chance! I could follow them to the right place, and I would not have to say a word to them.

Storytelling Tip

If you describe the sights, smells, and sounds of the story, you will bring the story alive for the reader. Try to include one or two adjectives in your sentences. The more descriptive the information, the more the reader will connect with the story you are telling.

In the following example, the writer is telling a story about her first day in English class. Notice the underlined words. They add depth to the story by giving additional information.

I walked into the <u>noisy</u> classroom and looked for a place to sit down. In the back of the <u>well-lit</u> room, I saw an <u>old</u> <u>wooden</u> desk and walked toward it. After a few moments, the <u>anxious</u> students quieted down when they observed the <u>prim</u> English teacher enter the room.

The Conclusion

Like academic essays, narrative essays need to have concluding ideas. In the **conclusion**, you finish describing the action in the essay. The final sentence can have two functions:

1. It can deliver the moral of the story by telling the reader what the character(s) learned from the experience.

2. It can make a prediction or a revelation (disclosure of something that was not known before) about future actions that will happen as a result of the events in the story.

Look at these examples:

Moral   The little boy had finally learned that telling the truth was the most important thing to do.

Prediction   I can only hope that one day I will be able to do the same for another traveler who is suffering through a terrible journey.

Revelation   Every New Year's Eve, my wife and I return to that magical spot and remember the selfless act that saved our lives.

✎ Writer's Note

Effective Narrative Essays

These are a few of the elements in an effective narrative essay:

*   a thesis that sets up the action in the introduction

*   transition sentences that connect events and help the reader follow the story

*   a conclusion that ends the story action and provides a moral, prediction, or revelation

Example Narrative Essay

A good way to learn what a narrative essay looks like is to read and study an example. In the next activity, you will read and study the content and organization of an example essay.

ACTIVITY 2 Studying an Example Essay

Discuss the questions that come before the example essay with a partner. Then read the essay. Work with a partner to answer the questions after the essay.

In this narrative essay, a traveler has a frustrating experience at an airport.

1. Have you ever had trouble trying to get to someplace very important? Where were you going? Why were you having problems?

2. What is a hero? What do you consider to be a heroic act?

Frustration at the Airport

1   I had never been more anxious in my life. I had just spent the last three endless hours trying to get to the airport so that I could travel home. Now, as I watched the bus driver set my luggage on the airport sidewalk, I realized that my frustration had only just begun.

2   This was my first visit to the international section of the airport, and nothing was familiar. I could not make sense of all the signs. Where was the ticket counter? Where should I take my luggage? I had no idea where the customs line was. I began to panic. What time was it? Where was my airplane? I had to find help because I could not be late!

frustration: a feeling of impatience and discouragement

3   I tried to ask a passing businessman for help, but all my words came out wrong. He just **scowled** and walked away. What had happened? I had been in this country for a whole semester, and I could not even remember how to ask for directions. This was awful! Another bus arrived at the **terminal**, and the passengers came out carrying all sorts of luggage. Here was my chance! I could follow them to the right place, and I would not have to say a word to them.

4   I dragged my enormous suitcase behind me and followed the group. We finally got to the elevators. Oh, no!! They all fit in it, but there was not enough room for me. I watched in **despair** as the elevator doors closed. I had no idea what to do next. I got on the elevator when it returned to the floor I was on and **gazed** at all the buttons. Which one could it be? I pressed button 3. The elevator slowly climbed up to the third floor and **jerked** to a stop. A high, squeaking noise announced the opening of the doors, and I looked around **timidly**.

5   Tears formed in my eyes as I saw the **deserted** lobby and realized that I would miss my airplane. Just then an old airport employee **shuffled** around the corner. He saw that I was lost and asked if he could help. He gave me his handkerchief to dry my eyes as I related my **predicament**. He smiled kindly, took me by the hand, and led me down a long hallway. We walked up some stairs, turned a corner, and, at last, there was customs! He led me past all the lines of people and pushed my luggage to the inspection counter.

6   When I turned to thank him for all his help, he was gone. I will never know that wonderful man's name, but I will always remember his unexpected **courtesy**. He helped me when I needed it the most. I can only hope that one day I will be able to do the same for another traveler who is suffering through a terrible journey.

scowl: to frown
a terminal: an arrival and departure point
　 for some forms of mass transportation
despair: the condition of having no hope
gaze: to look at slowly and steadily
jerk: to move with an abrupt motion

timidly: hesitantly, shyly
deserted: empty
shuffle: to walk by sliding one's feet along
　 the ground
a predicament: a troubling situation
a courtesy: a kind or polite action

✎ Writer's Note

Verb Tense in Narrative Essays

　　Most narrative essays are written in the simple past tense because narratives usually tell events that have already happened.

3. What is the narrative hook? _____

_____

4. Do you think the hook is effective? In other words, did it grab your attention? Why, or why not?

_____

_____

5. Where is the setting of this story?

_____

6. What is the theme, or the basic idea, of "Frustration at the Airport"?

_____

_____

7. Read the final sentences in Paragraphs 2, 3, 4, and 5. How does each one prepare the reader for the action to come?

_____

_____

8. What do you think the mood of the story is? What feeling or atmosphere does the writer create?

_____

_____

9. List the characters in this essay.

_____

10. What verb tense is used in "Frustration at the Airport"? _____ Write five verbs that the

writer uses. _____

_____

11. Is the story arranged in chronological order? In a few words, describe what happens first, second, third, and so on.

_____

_____

_____

12. Underline the transitional sentences.

13. Does the story end with a moral, prediction, or revelation? _____ Write the final sentence here.

_____

_____

✎ Building Better Sentences

Correct and varied sentence structure is essential to the quality of your writing. For further practice with "Frustration at the Airport," go to Practice 8 on page 169 in Appendix 1.

Below is an outline for "Frustration at the Airport." Some of the information is missing. Reread the essay beginning on page 41 and complete the outline.

Title: _____

I. Introduction (Paragraph 1)

   A. Hook: I had never been more anxious in my life. I had just spent the last three endless hours trying to get to the airport so that I could travel home.

   B. Thesis statement: _____

   _____

II. Body

   A. Paragraph 2 (Event 1) topic sentence: This was my first visit to the international section of the airport, and nothing was familiar.

   SUPPORT

   1. The signs were confusing.

   2. I began to panic.

   3. Transition sentence: _____

   _____

   B. Paragraph 3 (Event 2) topic sentence: _____

   _____

   SUPPORT

   1. He scowled and walked away.

   2. I could not remember how to ask for directions.

   3. _____

   4. Transition sentence: _____

   _____

   C. Paragraph 4 (Event 3) topic sentence: I dragged my enormous suitcase behind me and followed the group.

   SUPPORT

   1. _____

   2. I got on the elevator and looked at the buttons.

   3. _____

   4. Transition sentence: _____

   _____

D. Paragraph 5 (Event 4) topic sentence: Tears formed in my eyes as I saw the deserted lobby and realized that I would miss my airplane.

SUPPORT

    1. An airport employee offered to help.

    2. _____

    3. _____

    4. Transition sentence: He led me past all the lines of people and pushed my luggage to the inspection counter.

III. Conclusion (Paragraph 6)

    A. Close of the action: _____

    B. I will never know his name, but I will always remember his unexpected courtesy.

    C. _____

    D. Final sentence (moral, prediction, or revelation): _____

    _____

ACTIVITY 4 Adding Supporting Information

The following narrative essay is missing large parts of the story (supporting information in the body). As you read, add information that moves the story along. Be sure to write transition sentences at the end of Paragraphs 2, 3, and 4. If you need more space, use a separate piece of paper. Be as creative as you like!

EXAMPLE ESSAY 9

Making Your Own Luck

1   I should never have thrown the chain letter away. The letter clearly warned me that if I did, I would have one day of bad luck. I did not believe it, so I threw the silly piece of paper in the garbage. I thought the friend who sent me the letter was just a **superstitious** fool. Letters do not bring you luck. You make your own! That night, however, as I fell asleep, I had the uncomfortable feeling that something was not quite right.

2   When I woke up the next morning, I was surprised to find that I had overslept and would be late for work. As I rushed down the stairs to eat a quick breakfast, I **tripped** over my bag and

_____

_____

_____

_____

superstitious: irrational, believing in things that are not based on science   **trip:** to stumble or fall

3   On my way to work, I decided to take a shortcut through an old part of town.

_____

_____

_____

_____

4   When I arrived at work, I found a note on my desk from my boss. She wanted to see me **right away**. I took a deep breath and walked into her office. As I stepped inside, I noticed a scowl on her face.

_____

_____

_____

_____

5   Finally, after a long and difficult day, I returned home to find that my air conditioner was broken. I could not take it anymore! It had been the worst day of my life, and I did not want anything else to happen. I rushed to the garbage can and dug around for the chain letter I had thrown away the day before. It was covered with coffee grounds and potato peels, but I could still read the words: "Send ten copies of this letter to your friends and you will have good luck for a year." I sat down at the kitchen table and began to make copies for ten of my friends. They could take their chances, but I was not going to have any more bad luck!

right away: immediately

Building Better Sentences

Correct and varied sentence structure is essential to the quality of your writing. For further practice with "Making Your Own Luck," go to Practice 9 on page 170 in Appendix 1.

Language Focus

Connectors and Time Relationship Words

The most common way to organize events in a narrative essay is in chronological order. The event that occurs first is in the introduction, and the events that follow are in the next paragraphs (the body) and continue to the end (the conclusion).

To make sure that readers understand time relationships, effective writers of narrative essays use connecting words and phrases to show how events progress. Look at the lists of time words below. They contain some connectors that you can use in narrative writing. Brainstorm with your classmates to add more words to each list. (For a more complete list of connectors, see the Brief Writer's Handbook with Activities on pages 156–157.)

Chronological Order	Prepositions	Time Words That Begin Clauses*
first (second, third, etc.) next finally later now then	after (a moment) at (9:00 A.M.) by (bedtime, then) during (the afternoon) from (then on) until (five o'clock)	after as soon as before when while whenever until

*When time clauses occur at the beginning of a sentence, they MUST be followed by a comma.

ACTIVITY 5 Adding Connectors

Read the next essay. Fill in the blanks with an appropriate connector or time relationship word or phrase. Refer to the list in the Language Focus section above.

In this essay, the narrator tells about his friend's accident and what he (the narrator) learned from it.

EXAMPLE ESSAY 10

A Little Bit of Rest

1   I have always been an active person. I love to swim and play sports. I used to take **risks** when I

was having fun outdoors—until my good friend Mohayed had a little accident. _____

I am a lot more careful about what I do.

a risk: danger, a hazard

2   Mohayed has always been a biking **enthusiast**. He loves to ride his bright red mountain bike in the hills outside of our town to get his daily workout. One day during a rainstorm, he went out into the hills to ride his bike. The trails are very muddy and dangerous when it rains, but he did not let that stop him. _____ he was riding down the steepest hill on the trail, he lost control of his bike. The bike **skidded** in the mud, and he flipped over the handlebars. _____ he hit the ground, he landed on a large rock. He was hurt pretty badly, and he had to be rushed to the emergency room in an ambulance.

3   _____ he got there, the nurses quickly cleaned his cuts and scratches. _____ they took him to get X-rays of both his legs and his shoulder. After that, Mohayed saw the doctor, who said that he was lucky. Even though he was bruised all over, only his shoulder was broken. _____ the doctor put a big, clumsy-looking cast on Mohayed's shoulder. He told Mohayed that he would have to rest for the next six weeks so that his body could **heal** properly.

4   Because Mohayed was usually so active, he could not stay still. One week _____ the accident, he decided that he had to take a walk. As he was walking along, he tripped on the uneven sidewalk and lost his balance. He fell forward and landed on his new cast, and he broke it in half! As a result, he hurt his shoulder even more badly. He had to have a new cast put on. While he was there, the doctor **scolded** him and told him he that could not do anything at all _____ his bones had healed completely!

5   Even though I like adventure almost as much as Mohayed does, I have to admit that I learned many things from his **misfortune**. _____, no matter how much you love to do something, you should always consider safety. _____, if you are hurt, you should do what the doctors tell you to or you might not recover well. _____, a little bit of rest and quiet time never hurt anyone!

an enthusiast: a fan   **scold:** to reprimand, yell at
skid: to slide   **a misfortune:** an unlucky event
heal: to get better (physically), recover

 For more practice with connectors and time relationship words, try Unit 2, Activity 3 and Activity 4 on the *Great Writing 4* Web site: elt.heinle.com/greatwriting

Building Better Sentences

Correct and varied sentence structure is essential to the quality of your writing. For further practice with "A Little Bit of Rest," go to Practice 10 on page 171 in Appendix 1.

Writer's Note

Sentence Variety with Time Words

Essays that are written using only one or two sentence patterns can be dull to read. Good writers try to include variety in their sentences. Here are two ways to add variety with time words.

1. Follow the time word *after* with a noun.

   Change   Marta studied engineering at the University of Charleston. She graduated in 2006. Then she got a job with Johnson and Rowe, a local engineering firm.

   to   Marta studied engineering at the University of Charleston. **After her graduation** in 2006, she got a job with Johnson and Rowe, a local engineering firm.

   Change   I walked up the stairs to the stage. I was so frightened to begin my speech that I could actually hear my teeth chattering. I remembered my deep breathing exercise, looked confidently at my audience, and began to speak.

   to   I walked up the stairs to the stage. I was so frightened to begin my speech that I could actually hear my teeth chattering. **After my breathing exercise**, I looked confidently at my audience and began to speak.

2. Follow *after*, *before*, *while*, and *when* with a gerund.*

   Change   A rare golden Sitka spruce was cut down by unknown vandals. It had been growing for more than three hundred years.

   to   **After growing** for more than three hundred years, a rare golden Sitka spruce was cut down by unknown vandals.

   Change   Joanna Cannon ran for mayor. She promised to lower property taxes.

   to   **While running** for mayor, Joanna Cannon promised to lower property taxes.

*A gerund is a verb form that ends in -*ing* and is used as a noun, such as *walking* and *studying*.

Read the following narrative essay. Then combine the sentences listed above the blanks into one sentence. You may add time words and other connectors to combine the ideas. Write the new sentence on the lines provided.

In this essay, the narrator remembers learning how to drive from her father.

Learning to Drive

1   I could not believe it. Driving laws in Ontario allowed teenagers to get their licenses at the age of sixteen! This was the only benefit I could think of having immigrated to this country. I thought about my cousins in Italy and how jealous they would be when I told them I had my license.

- My sixteenth birthday approached. I beamed with excitement. I beamed with anticipation.

a. <u>As my sixteenth birthday approached, I beamed with excitement and anticipation.</u>

I did not know at the time that the driving lessons that I learned in our old minivan would stay with me for the rest of my life.

2   My father was the obvious choice to be my driving instructor, so we set up a schedule. The first lesson took place in the **driveway**.

- I sat in the passenger seat. At the same time, he explained the devices in the car. He also explained their functions.

b. _____

_____

I was particularly frightened by the stick shift on the floorboard. However, my father patiently lectured on the different floor pedals, the turn signals, and, my favorite, the car horn.

3   For the next lesson, I sat in the driver's seat. At that time, it felt more like a **throne** than anything else. My father asked me to turn on the car and proceeded to guide me into reverse. As I let up on the clutch and pressed the gas, I felt the car starting to move backward. I was controlling this machine!

- I backed out of the driveway. I went into the **residential** street. I did this slowly and carefully.

c. _____

_____

After a few moments of confusion, I had the car sputtering forward in first gear.

a driveway: an area in front of a home where people park their cars

a throne: a special chair meant for nobility
residential: areas where people live, not commercial

4   Two weeks of lessons passed, and I was beginning to get bored with the scenery. My father navigated me around the block again and again. I was passing the same landmarks—the neighbor's house, the dead tree down the street, and the kids playing in the empty lot on the corner. When I could stand it no more, I asked to move to a busier street. "Tomorrow. I think you are ready," my father replied, his eyes twinkling with pride.

5   My emotions were in overdrive the next day. I was finally on a busy street.

- I shifted from first gear to second gear. There were no problems.

d. _____

_____

Then came third gear. When I reached the appropriate speed, I put the car into fourth. I was flying in the old minivan!

- My father's voice was deep. It was concerned. His voice broke my spell.

e. _____

_____

He said calmly, "Honey, there is a red light ahead." My spell was broken as I realized I was traveling far above the speed limit and heading toward a red light. All the information that I had learned in the previous weeks leaked out of my brain. I did not know how to react. I flew through the intersection while blaring my horn.

6   That night my father was **somber**. I was in tears. How lucky we had been not to have been hit by another car.

- I waited for him to reprimand me. He did not.

f. _____

_____

He knew that I was aware of the **severity** of my moving violation. It is now twenty years later, and I have not forgotten that day. In fact, every time I accidentally drive through a red light, I remember the emotions of a sixteen-year-old and the wisdom of a loving father.

somber: serious   **the severity:** seriousness

 For more practice with sentence variety, try Unit 2, Activity 5 on the *Great Writing 4* Web site: elt.heinle.com/greatwriting

Building Better Sentences

Correct and varied sentence structure is essential to the quality of your writing. For further practice with "Learning to Drive," go to Practice 11 on page 172 in Appendix 1.

Building Better Vocabulary

ACTIVITY 7 Word Associations

Circle the word or phrase that is most closely related to the word or phrase on the left. If necessary, use a dictionary to check the meaning of words you do not know.

1. a scowl	a happy face	an angry face
2. a predicament	trouble	good luck
3. to shuffle	feet	ears
4. to gaze	mouth	eyes
5. misfortune	a good thing	a bad thing
6. an enthusiast	excited about	bored by
7. somber	shady	serious
8. residential	offices	houses and apartments
9. to heal	studying	illnesses
10. to scold	negative	positive

ACTIVITY 8 Using Collocations

Fill in each blank with the word or phrase on the left that most naturally completes the phrase on the right. If necessary, use a dictionary to check the meaning of words you do not know.

1. ask / to ask	how _____ for help	
2. journey / lobby	a deserted _____	
3. feeling / letter	an uncomfortable _____	

4. through / down   to rush _____ the stairs

5. mountain / problem   a steep _____

6. by / on   to trip _____ something

7. do / make   to _____ sense of something

8. hungry / ticket   a _____ counter

9. say / tell   to _____ the truth

10. street / towel   an uneven _____

Developing Narrative Essays

There are a few strategies in particular that can help you write and edit your narrative essay, such as choosing a topic, brainstorming, and making an outline.

Choosing a Topic

When you write a narrative essay, it is important to keep in mind that smaller is better. The smaller the action or event you choose, the easier it will be to keep your readers' interest and describe the action fully. For example, it would be impossible to describe—in one essay—all the events that helped make you the person you are today. However, you could choose one event that made a difference in your life, such as your first job or a special award, and write an essay about that. At the same time, be careful that the topic you choose is not too small. For example, a story about how your little brother called you a name one day would not be a good topic for a narrative essay. There should be enough action to make a story of five or six paragraphs.

✎ Writer's Note

Topic Tip

When you think about topics, try to remember something exciting, difficult, wonderful, or frightening that has happened to you. Can this event be developed into an interesting narrative essay?

Ask Yourself Questions

To help you think of some possible topics for narrative essays, ask yourself questions. Use the following questions as a guide:

- When was an important time in my life?
- What has happened in my experience that I would enjoy writing about?
- Is there an event in my life that other people (readers) would enjoy hearing about?
- How did I feel about a particular experience?
- Who was involved?
- Why do I remember this event so strongly? What effect did it have on me?
- Did anything change because of this experience?
- What interesting experiences do I know of that happened to other people?

If you are able to answer some of these questions about a specific experience that you or someone else had, then you may have a topic for a narrative essay.

ACTIVITY 9 Choosing Topics

Look at the pairs of topics. Put an X next to the topic that is the better choice for a narrative essay.

1. _____ Your last year in high school

   _____ Your last day in high school

2. _____ A scary airplane ride to another city

   _____ A scary trip around the world

3. _____ Guidelines for buying a car

   _____ Buying your first car

4. _____ Important academic ceremonies that you have participated in

   _____ Your brother's embarrassing wedding ceremony

5. _____ What I did last New Year's Eve

   _____ What I did last year

For more practice with topics for narrative essays, try Unit 2, Activity 6 on the *Great Writing 4* Web site: elt.heinle.com/greatwriting

Take a few minutes to think about possible topics for a narrative essay. Write some ideas here.

_____

_____

_____

Brainstorming

Brainstorming is a process by which you generate ideas about essay topics. There are many ways to brainstorm for a narrative essay. Here you will take a brief look at three different ways to develop ideas for an essay.

1. **Ask *wh-* questions about your topic.** With this method, you begin with a general idea of the topic that you are interested in. Then ask the questions *Who? What? When? Where? Why?* and, in some cases, *How?* The answers to these questions will help clarify what you would like to write about. Here is an example:

General topic: Celebrating Women's Day

Questions: <u>Who</u> celebrates Women's Day? <u>What</u> is the history of this celebration? <u>When</u> does the celebration take place? In <u>what</u> parts of the world is Women's Day celebrated? <u>Why</u> is it celebrated? <u>How</u> do people celebrate women on this day?

2. **Make a list of words or phrases that describe your topic.** This list can help with vocabulary choices when you write your essay. Here is a sample list on the topic of Women's Day:

springtime	flowers	warm weather
gifts	history	tradition
respect	candy	men give to women

3. **Make a visual map of your essay ideas.** One kind of visual map is called **clustering**. To cluster, write your topic in the center of a piece of paper and then circle it. On lines that come out from the circle, begin writing words and ideas associated with the topic. Write whatever comes to mind. Connect any words that are related. When you are finished, you will have many new ideas about your topic. Here is an example of clustering on the topic of Women's Day:

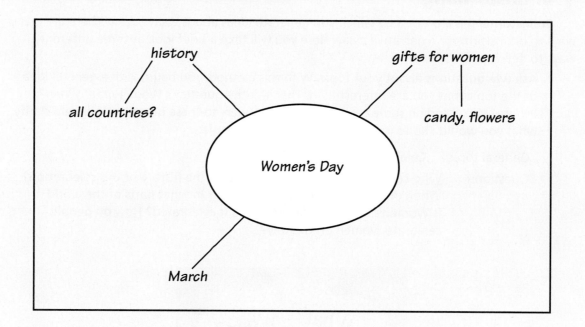

Writer's Note

Brainstorming Tips

Remember these important points about brainstorming:

- Choose a topic that you can write about in approximately five or six paragraphs.

- Choose a topic that is important to you—your essay will be easier to write and more interesting to read if you do.

- When you brainstorm, do not worry about correct grammar or spelling. Just focus on getting your ideas on paper.

Original Student Writing: Narrative Essay

ACTIVITY 11 Developing Narrative Ideas

Follow the steps below to develop ideas for a narrative essay.

1. Choose a topic that is suitable for a narrative essay. You may want to look at your notes from Activity 10 to help you. Remember that in a narrative essay, you tell a story. Work with other students to see if your topic is appropriate.

2. After you have a suitable topic, brainstorm some ideas about your topic. Use a separate piece of paper.

3. Now it is time to begin organizing your ideas. Remember that it is not necessary to tell every detail of the story. Include only the most important actions or events that move the story forward. Write some ideas here.

   a. Introduction (beginning of the story): theme, setting, and characters

   What is the basic idea of the story? Where does the story take place? When does the story take place? Who is in the story?

   _____

   _____

   _____

   b. Body (middle of the story): mood and plot

   What feeling or atmosphere do you want to create in your story? What will happen in the story?

   _____

   _____

   _____

   c. Conclusion (end of the story): end of the action, moral, prediction, or revelation

   What will happen last in your story? How will you wrap up the action of the story? Will your narrative essay have a moral, make a prediction, or provide a revelation?

   _____

   _____

   _____

ACTIVITY 12 Planning with an Outline

Use the outline below as a guide to help you make a more detailed plan for your narrative essay. You may need to use either more or fewer points under each heading. Include your ideas from Activity 11. Where possible, write in complete sentences.

Topic: ______________________________

I. Introduction (Paragraph 1)

A. Hook: ______________________________

____

B. Connecting information: ______________________________

____

____

C. Thesis statement: ______________________________

____

II. Body

A. Paragraph 2 (Event 1) topic sentence: ______________________________

____

SUPPORT

1. ______________________________
2. ______________________________
3. Transition sentence: ______________________________

____

B. Paragraph 3 (Event 2) topic sentence: ______________________________

____

SUPPORT

1. ______________________________
2. ______________________________
3. Transition sentence: ______________________________

____

C. Paragraph 4 (Event 3) topic sentence: _____

_____

   1. _____

   2. _____

   3. Transition sentence: _____

_____

D. Paragraph 5 (Event 4) topic sentence: _____

_____

   1. _____

   2. _____

   3. Transition sentence: _____

_____

III. Conclusion (Paragraph 6)

A. Close of the action: _____

_____

B. _____

_____

C. _____

_____

D. Final sentence (moral, prediction, or revelation): _____

_____

About Peer Editing

Many students think that writing a paper once is enough. This is rarely true. Even skilled and professional writers write and edit more than one draft.

Think of the first draft of your essay as your first attempt. Before you rewrite it, it is helpful to let someone read your paper, offer comments, and ask questions about your meaning. Many writers do not always see their weak areas, but a reader can help you see where you need to make improvements.

Sometimes you need more than one opinion about your essay. In class, peer editing is an easy way to get opinions. With this method, other students (your peers) read your essay and make comments using a set of questions and guidelines from the Peer Editing Sheets in Appendix 2. You will read someone else's essay, too. Peer editing can help you improve any areas that are not strong or clear up any areas that seem confusing to the reader.

Writer's Note

Suggestions for Peer Editing

- **Listen carefully.** In peer editing, you will receive many comments and some suggestions from other students. It is important to listen carefully to comments about your writing. You may think that what you wrote is clear and accurate, but readers can often point out places that need improvement. Remember that the comments are about the writing, not about you!

- **Make helpful comments.** When you read your classmates' essays, choose your words and comments carefully so that you do not hurt their feelings. For example, instead of saying, "This is bad grammar," be more specific and say, "You need to make sure that every sentence has a verb." Instead of saying, "I cannot understand any of your ideas," write a note that is more specific, such as, "What do you mean in this sentence?"

ACTIVITY 13 Peer Editing Your Outline

Exchange books with a partner and look at Activity 12. Read your partner's outline. Then use Peer Editing Sheet 1 on page 185 to help you comment on your partner's outline. Use your partner's feedback to revise your outline. Make sure you have enough information to develop your supporting sentences.

ACTIVITY 14 Writing a Narrative Essay

Write a narrative essay based on your revised outline from Activity 13. Use at least five of the vocabulary words or phrases presented in Activity 7 and Activity 8. Underline these words and phrases in your essay. Be sure to refer to the seven steps in the writing process in the Brief Writer's Handbook with Activities on pages 131–138.

ACTIVITY 15 Peer Editing Your Essay

Exchange papers from Activity 14 with a partner. Read your partner's writing. Then use Peer Editing Sheet 2 on pages 187–188 to help you comment on your partner's writing. Be sure to offer positive suggestions and comments that will help your partner improve his or her writing. Consider your partner's comments as you revise your own writing.

Additional Topics for Writing

Here are more ideas for topics for a narrative essay. Before you write, be sure to refer to the seven steps in the writing process in the Brief Writer's Handbook with Activities, pages 131–138.

TOPIC 1:   Write a story about a time in your life when you felt extremely proud of yourself. What were the circumstances? What was your accomplishment? Did you learn anything from this experience?

TOPIC 2:   Think of a person that you know well. Be sure that you feel comfortable writing about him or her. Tell a story about this person. What unusual or exciting experience has this person had? How did he or she influence you?

TOPIC 3:   Write about an important event in history from the point of view of someone who lived at that time.

TOPIC 4:   Choose a piece of music and listen to it. When you hear the music, what do you imagine is happening? Create a story that describes what is happening in the music.

TOPIC 5:   Think back to your childhood and a time when you were punished for doing something wrong. Write a narrative about that event, including what you did, who you were with, and how you were punished.

Timed Writing

How quickly can you write in English? There are many times when you must write quickly, such as on a test. It is important to feel comfortable during those times. Timed-writing practice can make you feel better about writing quickly in English.

First, read the essay guidelines below. Then take out a piece of paper. Read the writing prompt below the guidelines. As quickly as you can, brainstorm some ideas about this essay topic. You should spend <u>no more than</u> 5 minutes on brainstorming.

You will then have 40 minutes to write a 5-paragraph narrative essay about your topic. At the end of the 40 minutes, your teacher will collect your work and return it to you at a later date.

Narrative Essay Guidelines

- Remember to give your essay a title.

- Double-space your essay.

- Write as legibly as possible (if you are not using a computer).

- Include a short introduction that serves as background information, three body paragraphs that tell the narrative, and an appropriate conclusion.

- Try to give yourself a few minutes before the end of the activity to review your work. Check for spelling, verb tense, and subject-verb agreement mistakes.

> Narrate a story about a disagreement you had with a friend (or family member) and how the disagreement was resolved.

Comparison Essays

GOAL: To learn how to write a comparison essay

*Language Focus: Connectors for comparison essays

You make comparisons between things all the time. Whenever you make a decision, you have to compare your options. What will you eat for breakfast—cereal or a bagel? Where will you live—in an apartment or a dormitory? What will you study at the university—physics or mathematics? In order to make a decision, you need to look at the merits of each choice. You compare their differences and similarities. Then you choose the best option.

What Is a Comparison Essay?

In a **comparison essay**, you can compare ideas, people, countries, or other things. The subjects of this kind of essay are two items that are related in some way. You can focus on the similarities between the two items, on the differences, or on both the similarities and the differences. Your goal is to show your readers how these items are similar or different, what their strengths and weaknesses are, or what their advantages and disadvantages are. In a history class, your essay might compare the French Revolution and the American Revolution. In an economics class, you might write about the similarities and differences between capitalism and socialism. In an art class, you might write about the differences in the works of two impressionist painters, such as Monet and Renoir.

Like other essays, the comparison essay has an introductory paragraph that contains a hook and a thesis statement, three or four (or more) paragraphs that make up the body, and a concluding paragraph. (See Unit 1 for a review of the structure of an essay.)

Patterns of Organization

There are two basic ways to organize a comparison essay—the block method and the point-by-point method.

Block Method

With the **block method**, you present one subject and all its points of comparison before you do the same for the second subject. With this organization, you discuss each subject completely without interruption. Here is an example of the organization of a comparison essay about the social behavior of Russians and Mexicans.

Introduction	Paragraph 1	Hook, thesis
Body	Paragraphs 2 and 3	Russian social behavior • at parties • in school • at home
	Paragraphs 4 and 5	Mexican social behavior • at parties • in school • at home
Conclusion	Paragraph 6	Restated thesis, opinion

NOTE: Paragraphs 2 and 3 could be combined into one paragraph (paragraph 2); paragraphs 4 and 5 could also become one paragraph (paragraph 3). In this case, the conclusion would be paragraph 4.

Point-by-Point Method

With the **point-by-point method**, you present both subjects as they each relate to one point of comparison before moving on to the next point of comparison. Here is an example of the topic of the social behavior of Russians and Mexicans, using the point-by-point method of organization.

Introduction	Paragraph 1	Hook, thesis
Body	Paragraph 2	At parties • Russian social behavior • Mexican social behavior
	Paragraph 3	In school • Russian social behavior • Mexican social behavior
	Paragraph 4	At home • Russian social behavior • Mexican social behavior
Conclusion	Paragraph 5	Restated thesis, opinion

With both the point-by-point and the block methods, the writer sometimes ends with an opinion as to which of the two subjects is preferable.

 For practice with topics for comparison essays, try Unit 3, Activity 1, on the *Great Writing 4* Web site: elt.heinle.com/greatwriting

Parallel Organization of Supporting Information

In the block-method example, notice that the supporting information in Paragraphs 2 and 3 includes behavior at parties, school, and home. The supporting information in Paragraphs 4 and 5 also includes these three aspects of behavior. In the point-by-point method, the supporting information includes behavior at parties, school, and home as well, but information about the behavior of both cultures is presented in one setting before going on to discuss both cultures' behavior in the next setting.

These repeated structures are called parallel organization. No matter which overall method of organization you choose, parallel organization is required of your information in all comparison essays.

Choosing a Method of Organization

How do you know which method of organization is better for your comparison essay? Consider the following information about each method.

Block method:

- You develop one subject completely, without interruption, before describing the second subject.

- It may be difficult for readers to see the parallel points of comparison between your two subjects. Some rereading or more critical reading of certain parts of the essay may be necessary.

Point-by-point method:

- Both subjects are presented in each paragraph, so readers go back and forth between the two subjects.

- The parallel points of comparison may be easier to see.

As you decide which method to use, consider your subjects. Ask yourself how complex the two items you are comparing are. Think about your readers. Ask yourself which method would make it easier for them to follow your ideas about these particular subjects. Also, consider your writing style. Which organization method are you more comfortable with?

Example Comparison Essay

A good way to learn how to write a comparison essay is to study an example. In the next activity, you will read and study the content and organization of an example essay.

Discuss the questions that come before the example comparison essay with a partner. Then read the essay. Work with a partner to answer the questions after the essay.

In this essay, the writer compares some features of Brazil and the United States.

1. What do you know about the different cultural groups who live in Brazil and the United States?
2. What does the word *individualism* mean to you?

EXAMPLE ESSAY 12

Not as Different as You Think

1   All countries in the world are unique. Obviously, countries are different from one another in location, size, culture, government, climate, and lifestyles. However, many countries share some surprising similarities. Some may think that because Brazil and the United States are in different **hemispheres**, these two nations have nothing in common. On the contrary, they share many similarities.

2   One important similarity is their size. Both Brazil and the United States are large countries. Brazil covers almost half of the South American continent. Few Brazilians can say that they have traveled **extensively** within the country's borders. Because of Brazil's large size, its weather varies greatly from one area to another. Like Brazil, the United States takes up a significant portion of its continent (North America), so most Americans have visited only a few of the 50 states. In addition, the United States has a wide range of **climates**. When the Northeast is experiencing snowstorms, cities like Miami, Florida, can have temperatures over 85 degrees Fahrenheit.

3   Another similarity between Brazil and the United States is the **diversity** of ethnic groups. Brazil was colonized by Europeans, and its culture has been greatly influenced by this fact. However, the identity of the Brazilian people is not **solely** a product of Western civilization. Brazil is a "melting pot" of many ethnic groups that immigrated there and mixed with the native people. The United States also has a diversity of ethnic groups representing the early colonists from northern Europe as well as groups from Africa, the Mediterranean, Asia, and South America. The mixture of cultures and **customs** has worked to form ethnically rich cultures in both countries.

a hemisphere: one half of the world
extensively: widely, over a large area
climate: the usual weather of a region over a period of time

diversity: variety
solely: exclusively
a custom: a learned social or cultural behavior

4 Finally, **individualism** is an important value for both Brazilians and Americans. Brazil works hard to defend the **concept** of freedom of choice. Citizens believe that they have the right to do and be whatever they desire as long as they do not hurt others. Individualism and freedom of choice also exist in the United States, where freedom is perhaps the highest value of the people. Some people may believe that the desire for individual expression is divisive and can make a country weak. However, the ability of people to be whatever they want makes both countries strong.

5 Although Brazil and the United States are unique countries, there are **remarkable** similarities in their size, ethnic diversity, and personal values. Some people tend to believe that their culture and country are without equal. Nevertheless, it is important to remember that people as a whole have more in common than they generally think they do.

individualism: uniqueness, independence   **remarkable:** amazing, extraordinary
a concept: an idea

3. What two subjects does the writer compare in this essay?

_____

4. What method of organization does the writer use—point-by-point or block?

_____

5. What is the hook for this essay? Write it here.

_____

_____

_____

6. Underline the thesis statement. Is the thesis restated in the conclusion (Paragraph 5)? If yes, underline the sentence in the conclusion that restates the thesis.

7. In Paragraph 2, the author writes about the ways in which size affects Brazil and the United States. In the following chart, list the supporting information the writer uses.

The Effects of Size

Brazil	United States
1. _____	1. _____
_____	_____
2. _____	2. _____
_____	_____
3. _____	3. _____
_____	_____

8. Reread the concluding paragraph of "Not as Different as You Think." Does the writer offer a

   suggestion, an opinion, or a prediction? _____ Write the concluding sentence here.

   _____

   _____

🔨 Building Better Sentences

Correct and varied sentence structure is essential to the quality of your writing. For further practice with "Not as Different as You Think," go to Practice 12 on page 173 in Appendix 1.

Developing Comparison Essays

In this next section, you will develop comparison essays as you make an outline, write supporting information, and study connectors. In the following activities, you will practice the skills you need to write an effective comparison essay.

ACTIVITY 2 Outlining Practice

Below is a specific outline for "Not as Different as You Think." (For a review of specific outlines, see pages 28–32.) Some of the information is missing. Reread the essay beginning on page 65 and complete the outline.

Title: _____

   I. Introduction (Paragraph 1)

       A. Hook: <u>All countries in the world are unique.</u>

B. Connecting information: Different location, size, culture, government, climate, lifestyle

C. Thesis statement: _____

_____

II. Body

A. Paragraph 2 (Similarity 1) topic sentence: _____

_____

1. Brazil's characteristics

   a. Size: _____

   b. Travel: Few Brazilians have traveled extensively in their country.

   c. Climate: _____

2. _____

   a. _____

   b. Travel: _____

   c. Climate: The weather can be extremely different in the northern and the southern parts of the country.

B. Paragraph 3 (Similarity 2) topic sentence: Another similarity is the diversity of ethnic groups.

1. Brazil

   a. _____

   b. Other ethnic groups

   c. _____

2. United States

   a. Europe

   b. Africa

   c. the Mediterranean

   d. _____

   e. _____

SUPPORT

SUPPORT

C. Paragraph 4 (Similarity 3) topic sentence: _____

_____

   1. Brazilians' belief in freedom: _____

     _____

   2. _____

     _____

III. Conclusion (Paragraph 5)

  A. Restated thesis: _____

    _____

  B. Opinion: Nevertheless, it is important to remember that people as a whole have more in common than they generally think they do.

✎ Writer's Note

Asking Questions

How can you develop details and facts that will support your main ideas (topic sentences) in each paragraph? One of the best ways to write this supporting information is to ask yourself questions about the topic—*Where? Why? When? Who? What? How?*

ACTIVITY 3 Supporting Information

The following comparison essay is missing the supporting information. As you read the essay, work with a partner to write supporting sentences for each paragraph. If you need more space, use a separate piece of paper. After you finish, compare your supporting information with that of other students. (Note: This essay follows the point-by-point organizational pattern.)

What factors are most important to you and your family when buying a car?

Transportation Decisions for Families

1   Transportation today is much different from the way that it was 50 years ago. At that time, people who wanted to buy an automobile had a small variety to choose from. Nowadays, there are so many choices that it could take months to look at all the cars on the market. For those buyers who are looking for a vehicle for their families, one of the first questions is, "Should I buy a sports utility vehicle (SUV) or a four-door sedan?" To reach a decision, a buyer can compare these two car types in terms of their overall cost, convenience, and style.

2   SUVs and sedans often differ in their costs. _____

_____

_____

_____

_____

_____

_____

3   Another thing to consider is the convenience factor. _____

_____

_____

_____

_____

_____

_____

4   Finally, there is the subject of style. _____

_____

_____

_____

_____

_____

_____

5   All cars are used for transportation, but it is important to remember that, depending on the car category, there are differences in cost, convenience, and style. Choosing between an SUV and a four-door sedan is a personal decision for you and your family. Careful consideration of the information presented here will make choosing a car less complicated.

Correct and varied sentence structure is essential to the quality of your writing. For further practice with "Transportation Decisions for Families," go to Practice 13 on page 174 in Appendix 1.

Language Focus

Connectors for Comparison Essays

Writers use **connectors** in a well-organized essay to help clarify their main ideas. Connectors help readers by providing logical connections between sentences, ideas, and paragraphs. Notice that when these words, and often the phrase that follows them, begin a sentence, they are followed by a comma.

The following two charts show connectors that can be used in comparison essays. Notice that the first chart is for comparison words and phrases and the second chart is for contrast words and phrases. (For a more complete list of connectors, see the Brief Writer's Handbook with Activities, pages 156–157.)

Connectors That Show Comparison	
Between sentences or paragraphs	**Example**
In addition,	Both Red Beauty and Midnight Dream roses are known for the size of their blooms, their color, and their fragrance. **In addition**, they are easy to grow.
Similarly,	The Midnight Dream rose won awards in local contests last year. **Similarly**, the Red Beauty rose was singled out for its beauty.
Likewise,	The blooms of Red Beauty roses last longer than those of most other roses. **Likewise**, the blooms of the Midnight Dream rose are long-lasting.
Compared to . . . ,	Some roses last for a very short time. **Compared to** these roses, the blooms of Red Beauty and Midnight Dream roses last a long time.

Connectors That Show Contrast	
Between sentences or paragraphs	**Example**
However, / On the other hand,	Many differences are clear to even novice gardeners. **However / On the other hand,** some of their differences are not very obvious.
In contrast,	Red Beauty has a strong, sweet fragrance. **In contrast,** Midnight Dream's fragrance is light and fruity.
Although . . . ,	Both Midnight Dream roses and Red Beauty roses are red. **Although** both these two varieties have red flowers, Midnight Dream roses are much darker than Red Beauty roses.
Even though . . . ,	Red Beauty roses and Midnight Dream roses are long-stemmed roses. **Even though** both these two species are long-stemmed roses, Red Beauty stems are thin and covered with thorns while Midnight Dream stems are thick and have almost no thorns.
Unlike . . . ,	What do we know about the cost of these two kinds of roses? **Unlike** Red Beauty, Midnight Dream roses are relatively inexpensive.

ACTIVITY 4 Connectors

Read the following student essay and circle the appropriate connector in each set of parentheses. Refer to the list in the Language Focus section on pages 71–72, if necessary.

The writer in this essay compares the university entrance requirements in Taiwan before and after 2001 when educational reforms were implemented.

Higher Education Reforms in Taiwan

1   I completed my university studies less than ten years ago in Taiwan. (However/Another), I cannot consider myself a **product** of modern Taiwanese education. If people ask me about the current educational system in Taiwan, I do not have an easy answer for them. As it happens, Taiwan experienced many educational reforms in 2001. The changes focused on the steps needed to enter a Taiwanese university. In short, the entry requirements then and now have changed in three major areas: testing, non-academic activities, and school **autonomy**.

2   One of the most obvious differences between entry into college before and now is the entrance test **criterion**. When I was a student, there was one and only one exam that all high school students took. If a student did well on the exam, his or her future as a university student was **set**. If the exam result was low, that student had little, if any, opportunity to get a higher education. This "high stakes" exam mentality did much damage to many of my classmates. (In addition/ However), the school reforms of 2001 changed that. Nowadays, Taiwanese students get more than one opportunity to take the test. In addition, universities are now using testing options, including standardized tests that are commonly utilized in the United States and tests that focus on critical thinking and leadership skills. (Unlike/Even though) students in the past, Taiwanese students today are assessed based on much more than rote learning and information.

3   (However/In addition), there is a great difference in the importance of non-academic **achievements** for college entry. Before 2001, external activities such as membership in clubs and other areas were not considered at all in evaluating a student's worthiness. Again, the focus was solely on the student's examination score. (In contrast/Likewise), the current educational requirements in Taiwan are much broader. A Taiwanese student today can be evaluated on his or her outside activities—not just his or her academic achievements—from high school. This **paradigm** shift ends up affecting not only the student's eventual entry to a university but also his or her high school experience.

a product: a creation
autonomy: self-rule; independence
a criterion: a condition; a standard (plural: *criteria*)

set: established, ready
an achievement: a success, an accomplishment
a paradigm: a model; an archetype

4   The last obvious difference between the old and new educational systems in Taiwan is the autonomy of each university in making enrollment choices. Prior to 2001, universities relied on the entrance exam. There was little variation from one school to another in terms of evaluating prospective students. (Even though/Compared to) these universities claimed to pay some attention to the "whole" student, in reality the focus was on the exam. (In contrast/Likewise), Taiwanese universities today can be completely unique and creative in their acceptance procedures. Admissions offices can prepare their own unique examinations, develop special projects for students to complete, and even accept letters of recommendation from high schools. Universities now have the authority to decide how they will assess their prospective students.

5   Education is **vital** to everyone's future success. While it may take ten years to grow a tree, a **sound** educational system may take twice as long to take root. (However/Although) my education differed tremendously from the education of Taiwanese students today, as students we both share the ultimate goal: to become as well educated as we can. This goal can be reached only if people take advantage of all the educational opportunities given to them.

vital: fundamental; essential   **sound:** reliable; firm; positive

 For more practice with connectors, try Unit 3, Activity 2 on the *Great Writing 4* Web site: elt.heinle.com/greatwriting

⚒ Building Better Sentences

Correct and varied sentence structure is essential to the quality of your writing. For further practice with "Higher Education Reforms in Taiwan," go to Practice 14 on page 175 in Appendix 1.

ACTIVITY 5 Word Associations

Circle the word or phrase that is most closely related to the word or phrase on the left. If necessary, use a dictionary to check the meaning of words you do not know.

1. diversity	difference		distance
2. customs	shirts		traditions
3. a concept	an idea		music
4. remarkable	repetitive		amazing
5. a hemisphere	in math class		in geography class
6. to take root	to begin to grow		to refuse to grow
7. solely	hardly		only
8. sound	misunderstood		solid
9. likewise	but		also
10. a climate	weather		yearly salary

ACTIVITY 6 Using Collocations

Fill in each blank with the word on the left that most naturally completes the phrase on the right. If necessary, use a dictionary to check the meaning of words you do not know.

1. make / pay   to_____ attention to something

2. on / to   to be vital _____ (the plan's success)

3. origin / root   to take _____

4. find / reach   to _____ a decision

5. at / in   the differences _____ size, cost, and color

6. advantage / time   to take _____ of

7. superior / ultimate our _____ goal

8. likewise / significant a _____ portion

9. common / contrary   to have nothing in _____

10. groups / people   ethnic _____

Developing Ideas for Writing

Brainstorming

You will be asked to write comparison essays in many of your classes. Often, you will be given the two subjects to be compared, such as two works of literature, two kinds of chemical compounds, or two political beliefs. When you have to choose your own subjects for comparison, the following brainstorming tips will help you.

Tips for Brainstorming Subjects

1. **The subjects should have something in common.** For example, soccer and hockey are both fast-paced games that require a player to score a point by putting an object into a goal guarded by a player from the other team.
2. **The two subjects must also have some differences.** For example, the most obvious differences between the two games are the playing field, the protective equipment, and the number of players.
3. **You need to have enough information on each topic to make your comparisons.** If you choose two sports that are not well-known, it might be more difficult to find information about them.

Make a List

A good way to determine whether you have enough information about similarities and differences between two subjects is to brainstorm a list. Read the information in the lists below.

Ice Hockey	Soccer
played on ice	played on a grass field
6 players on a team	11 players on a team
uses a puck	uses a soccer ball
very popular sport	very popular sport
players use lots of protective pads	players use some protective pads
cannot touch the puck with your hands	cannot touch the ball with your hands
goal = puck in the net	goal = ball in the net

As you can see, soccer and hockey have many similarities and a few differences. Notice that the similarities are circled. These are "links" between the two subjects. A writer could use these links to highlight the similarities between the two games or to lead into a discussion of the differences between them: "Although both soccer and hockey are popular, more schools have organized soccer teams than hockey . . . ."

Make a Venn Diagram

Another way to brainstorm similarities and differences is to use a Venn diagram. (Perhaps you have used Venn diagrams in math class.) A Venn diagram is a visual representation of the similarities and differences between two concepts. Here is a Venn diagram of the characteristics of hockey and soccer.

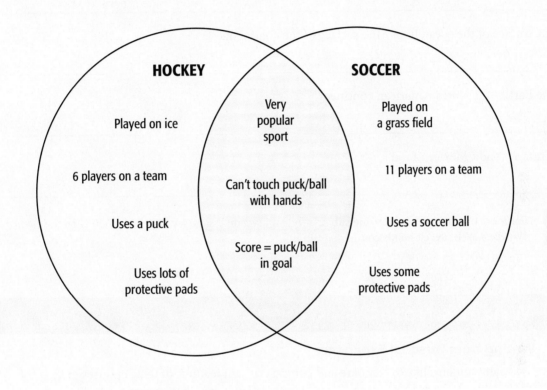

ACTIVITY 7 Identifying Good Subjects

Below are pairs of potential subjects for a comparison essay. Write yes *on the line under the pairs that would be good subjects and explain briefly what characteristics could be compared. Write* no *under the subjects that would not be good choices and change one or both of them into more suitable subjects. The first two have been done for you.*

1. living in a house / living in an apartment

   <u>yes—compare costs, privacy, space</u>

2. international travel / 747 airplanes

   <u>no—change "747 airplanes" to "domestic travel"</u>

3. high school / college

   _____

4. the weather in Toronto / tourist attractions in Toronto

_____

5. wild animals / animals in a zoo

_____

6. computers / computer keyboards

_____

7. hands / feet

_____

8. the surface of the ocean floor / the surface of the continents

_____

9. the Earth / the North American continent

_____

10. Chinese food / Mexican food

_____

 For more practice with identifying subjects for comparison essays, try Unit 3, Activity 3 on the *Great Writing 4* Web site: elt.heinle.com/greatwriting

Writer's Note

Writing from Personal Experience

   Many students like to compare and contrast certain features of their cultures to those of other cultures. These topics usually lead to interesting essays that engage readers.

Original Student Writing: Comparison Essay

ACTIVITY 8 Working with a Topic

Complete the following steps to develop ideas for a comparison essay.

   1. Choose one topic from the list below or use your own idea for a topic. If you want to use an original idea, talk to your teacher to see if it is appropriate for a comparison essay.

two sports	two movies	two systems of education
two places	two machines	two kinds of professions
two desserts	two famous people	two celebrations or holidays

2. Use the following chart to brainstorm a list of information about each subject. If you like, use the list about soccer and hockey on page 76 as a guide.

TOPIC: _____

Subject 1: _____	Subject 2: _____

3. Now fill in the Venn diagram using the information from the chart in Item 2 above.

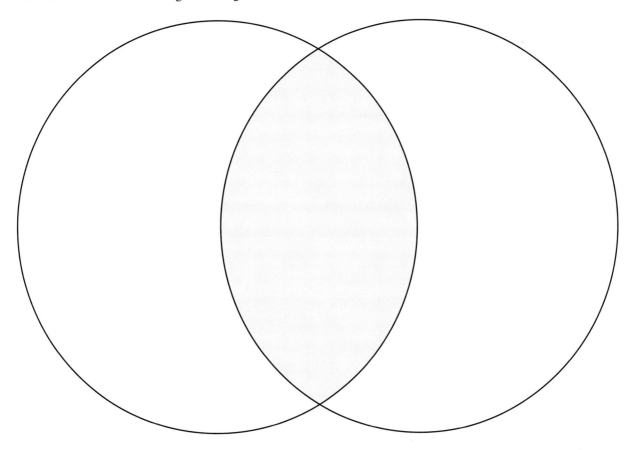

4. Decide if you are going to focus on the similarities or the differences between the two subjects or both in your comparison essay. Then choose three or four main points of comparison that you will use and list them here.

a. _____

b. _____

c. _____

d. _____

For more practice with Venn diagrams, try Unit 3, Activity 4, Activity 5, and Activity 6 on the *Great Writing 4* Web site: elt.heinle.com/greatwriting

Writer's Note

Ideas for Supporting Information

In the next activity, you will develop supporting information. Here are some ideas to use as supporting information in your body paragraphs:

- give descriptions
- give examples
- explain the causes
- explain the effects

ACTIVITY 9 Planning with an Outline

Use the following outline as a guide to help you brainstorm a more detailed plan for your comparison essay. For this activity, use the point-by-point method of organization. (See page 63.) Remember that the point-by-point method organizes each paragraph by one point of comparison, such as the languages, the populations, or the climates of two countries. Include your ideas from Activity 8. Write complete sentences where possible.

Topic: _____

I. Introduction (Paragraph 1)

A. Hook: _____

_____

B. Connecting information: _____

_____

_____

C. Thesis statement: _____

_____

_____

II. Body

    A. Paragraph 2 (first point of comparison) topic sentence: _____

    _____

        1. _____

            a. _____

            b. _____

        2. _____

            a. _____

            b. _____

    B. Paragraph 3 (second point of comparison) topic sentence: _____

    _____

        1. _____

            a. _____

            b. _____

        2. _____

            a. _____

            b. _____

    C. Paragraph 4 (third point of comparison) topic sentence: _____

    _____

        1. _____

            a. _____

            b. _____

        2. _____

            a. _____

            b. _____

III. Conclusion (Paragraph 5)

    A. Restated thesis: _____

    _____

    B. Suggestion, opinion, or prediction: _____

    _____

ACTIVITY 10 Peer Editing Your Outline

Exchange books with a partner and look at Activity 9. Read your partner's outline. Then use Peer Editing Sheet 3 on page 189 to help you comment on your partner's outline. Use your partner's feedback to revise your outline. Make sure you have enough information to develop your supporting sentences.

ACTIVITY 11 Writing a Comparison Essay

Write a comparison essay based on your revised outline from Activity 10. Use at least five of the vocabulary words or phrases presented in Activity 5 and Activity 6. Underline these words and phrases in your essay. Be sure to refer to the seven steps in the writing process in the Brief Writer's Handbook with Activities on pages 131–138.

ACTIVITY 12 Peer Editing Your Essay

Exchange papers from Activity 11 with a partner. Read your partner's writing. Then use Peer Editing Sheet 4 on page 191 to help you comment on your partner's writing. Be sure to offer positive suggestions and comments that will help your partner improve his or her writing. Consider your partner's comments as you revise your own writing.

Additional Topics for Writing

Here are more ideas for topics for a comparison essay. Before you write, be sure to refer to the seven steps in the writing process in the Brief Writer's Handbook with Activities, pages 131–138.

TOPIC 1: Compare a book to its movie version. How are the two similar and different? Are the characters and the plot the same? Do you like the movie or the book better? Explain your answer.

TOPIC 2: Compare the situation in a country before and after an important historical event, such as Cuba before and after Fidel Castro came to power.

TOPIC 3: Discuss two kinds of music, such as classical and pop. A few points of comparison might be artists, instruments, audiences, and popularity.

TOPIC 4: Show how the world has changed since the invention of the cell (mobile) phone. How did people communicate before its invention? How easy or difficult was it to get in contact with someone?

TOPIC 5: Show the similarities and differences in the ways that two cultures celebrate an important event, such as a birthday, wedding, or funeral.

How quickly can you write in English? There are many times when you must write quickly, such as on a test. It is important to feel comfortable during those times. Timed-writing practice can make you feel better about writing quickly in English.

First, read the essay guidelines below. Then take out a piece of paper. Read the writing prompt below the guidelines. As quickly as you can, write a basic outline for this writing prompt (including the thesis and your three main points). You should spend <u>no more than</u> 5 minutes on your outline.

You will then have 40 minutes to write a 5-paragraph comparison essay about your topic. At the end of the 40 minutes, your teacher will collect your work and return it to you at a later date.

Comparison Essay Guidelines

- Use the point-by-point method.

- Remember to give your essay a title.

- Double-space your essay.

- Write as legibly as possible (if you are not using a computer).

- Include a short introduction (with a thesis statement), three body paragraphs, and a conclusion.

- Try to give yourself a few minutes before the end of the activity to review your work. Check for spelling, verb tense, and subject-verb agreement mistakes.

> Compare two popular vacation destinations.

Cause-Effect Essays

GOAL: To learn how to write a cause-effect essay

Language Focus: Connectors for cause-effect essays

What Is a Cause-Effect Essay?

A **cause-effect essay** shows the reader the relationship between something that happens and its consequences or between actions and results. For example, if too much commercial fishing is allowed in the North Atlantic Ocean (action), the fish population in some areas may diminish or disappear (result). Cause-effect essays can be informative, analytical, and insightful.

In this unit, you will study two kinds of cause-effect essays. Very simply, in one method, the writer focuses on the <u>causes</u> of something. Just think of how many people, when they are given a piece of information, like to analyze the topic and ask the question *Why?* or *How?* This is called the **focus-on-causes** method. In the second method, the writer emphasizes the <u>effects</u> or results of a cause. People who like to think hypothetically—answering the question *What if?*—focus on the outcome of a particular event or action. These writers often write **focus-on-effects** essays.

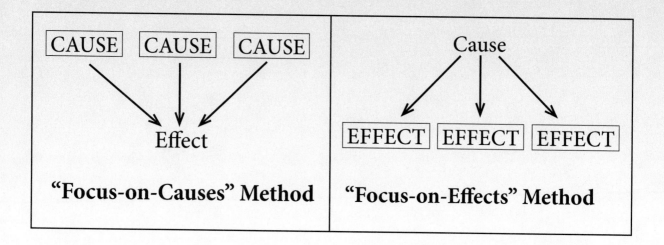

Imagine that your instructor gives you the following writing topic: quitting a job. You have the choice of using the focus-on-causes method or the focus-on-effects method.

Focus-on-causes method: You can choose to write an essay on why people quit their jobs and brainstorm possible reasons they may have for doing so. Each paragraph would contain a different cause.

Focus-on-effects method: On the other hand, you may want to emphasize the effects of quitting a job—perhaps detailing the emotional and financial consequences—in your body paragraphs. In this case, each paragraph would address one effect.

Writer's Note

Cause-Effect Essay Methods

The two cause-effect essay methods answer different questions.

Essays that use the focus-on-causes method answer the question, **"Why does something happen?"**	Essays that use the focus-on-effects method answer the question, **"What happens when . . . ?"**

For practice with topics for cause-effect essays, try Unit 4, Activity 1 on the *Great Writing 4* Web site: elt.heinle.com/greatwriting

Example Cause-Effect Essay

Studying example essays is a good way to learn how to write in a particular rhetorical style. In the next two activities, you will read and study the content and organization of an example essay.

ACTIVITY 1 Studying an Example Essay

Read the questions that come before the example essay and think about how you would answer them. Then discuss them with a partner or in a small group. Read the essay and then work with a partner to answer the questions after the essay.

This focus-on-causes essay answers the question, "Why do people lie?"

1. Why do you think people lie?

2. Is it ever acceptable to lie? Give examples of acceptable and unacceptable lies.

The Truth behind Lying

1   Most children are taught the virtue of honesty from fairy tales and other stories. The **celebrated** story of Pinocchio, who begins life as a **puppet**, teaches the importance of telling the truth. Every time Pinocchio lies, his nose grows longer and longer. Another story about the boy who "cried wolf" exemplifies how lying led to his losing all of his sheep as well as the trust of his fellow villagers. In the United States, young children study the tale of young George Washington, who finally admits to his father that he cut down a cherry tree. These types of stories typically show children that "honesty is the best policy." Still, if this is the case, then why do so many people lie? The fact is that human beings lie for many reasons.

2   One reason for lying has to do with minimizing a mistake. While it is true that everyone makes a **blunder** from time to time, some people do not have the courage to admit when they do because they might be blamed for the errors. For example, students might lie to their teachers about unfinished homework. They might say that they left the work at home when, in fact, they did not do the work at all. These students do not want to seem irresponsible, so they make up an excuse—a lie—to save face.

3   Another reason people lie is to get out of situations that they do not want to be in or cannot manage. For example, if a company decides to have a weekend meeting, one of the managers might not feel like attending. She may call her boss and give this excuse: "I've been fighting off a cold all week, and I truly cannot risk getting the others sick. I'll be sure to get all of the notes on Monday." When individuals do not want to admit the truth and then face the consequences, they use lies to **avoid** difficulties.

celebrated: famous, renowned
a puppet: a toy that is moved by strings

a blunder: a careless mistake
avoid: to keep away from

4   In contrast, some people might tell a "white lie" when they do not want to hurt someone else's feelings. For example, if a good friend shows up with an **unflattering** new haircut, one could be truthful and say, "That haircut looks awful. What were you thinking?!" A more likely scenario is to say, "It's very original! It suits you," and spare the friend's feelings. These types of lies are generally not considered negative or wrong. In fact, many people who have told the truth to loved ones, only to see the negative reaction, wish they *had* told a white lie. Therefore, white lies can be useful in maintaining good relationships.

5   A somewhat different reason for lying has to do with self-protection. Parents, particularly those with small children, may teach their children to use this type of "protective" lie in certain circumstances. What should children do if a stranger calls while the parents are out? Many parents teach their children to explain that mom and dad are too busy to come to the phone at that time. In this situation, protective lying can prevent harm or disaster.

6   People lie for many reasons, both good and bad. However, before people **resort to** lying in order to cover up mistakes or to avoid unpleasant situations, perhaps the motives for lying should be analyzed. One's lies may one day be exposed and cause severe embarrassment or the loss of people's trust.

unflattering: unattractive, not favorable   **resort to:** to do something only because other options have failed

3. What is the thesis statement? _____

    _____

4. What three examples of liars from famous stories does the author give in the introduction paragraph?

    a. _____

    b. _____

    c. _____

5. In Paragraph 4, the phrase *white lie* is used in the topic sentence but is not defined. Write your own

    definition of a white lie. _____

    _____

6. In Paragraph 5, the author supports the topic sentence by giving an example of a dangerous situation. What example does the author give?

    _____

    _____

7. Reread the concluding paragraph of "The Truth behind Lying." Does the writer offer a suggestion,

    an opinion, or a prediction? _____ Write the final sentence here.

    _____

    _____

Building Better Sentences

Correct and varied sentence structure is essential to the quality of your writing. For further practice with "The Truth behind Lying," go to Practice 15 on page 176 in Appendix 1.

ACTIVITY 2 Studying an Example Essay

Discuss the questions that come before the example essay with a partner. Then read the essay. Work with a partner to answer the questions after the essay.

This focus-on-effects essay discusses some of the effects of the breakup of the Soviet Union.

1. Do you remember the fall of the Soviet Union?
2. How many former Soviet Republics can you name?

EXAMPLE ESSAY 16

The Fall

1   For almost 50 years, the Cold War was one of the most talked about issues in international politics. Tensions between Western countries and the Soviet Union were high, and the world felt the **potential** danger of a disastrous conflict. When the Iron Curtain fell, many countries **rejoiced**. Independent-minded Soviet Republics got the independence they had wanted, and the communist **ideology** that had been so **prevalent** began to lose ground. About two decades after the breakup of the Soviet Union, the effects are still being felt.

potential: possible
rejoice: to celebrate

an ideology: a system of beliefs
prevalent: common, accepted

2   One of the most obvious changes in the post-communist world has been the **shift** to a market economy. Governments that once had **subsidized** the costs of basic necessities, such as food, transportation, housing, and electricity, are now letting competition and external factors determine the prices of these items. Inflation is high, and many citizens are having a difficult time adjusting to the **fluctuations** in prices based on supply and demand. However, imported goods are now commonplace in local markets, so consumers have more choices in what they buy. The switch to a market economy is often a painful process, but the citizens of the former Soviet Union are still confident that they will one day benefit financially from the economic changes.

3   Another anticipated effect of the fall of the Iron Curtain is **sovereignty**. The Soviet Union existed as one entity for many years, but now one can count a number of emerging republics, including Estonia, Latvia, Lithuania, Georgia, Ukraine, and Uzbekistan. These republics are currently in the process of shaping their own independent identities. They can focus on rebuilding their own cultures, languages, and priorities. This empowerment increases national pride and uniqueness. The idea of all Soviets being one and the same is now gone. Clearly, national identity is at the **forefront** of many people's minds.

4   While many former Soviets now feel a sense of national identity, the fall of the Soviet Union has taken away the identity of many others. Many ethnic groups have lived in this part of the world for generations. They were raised as Soviets, spoke Russian as a native language, and were taught to believe that they were citizens of the great superpower. Koreans, Tartars, Uighurs, and other ethnic groups can be found in most of the former Soviet Republics. Now that independence has spread from Eastern Europe to Central Asia, many of these citizens are considered minority groups. They do not want to be **repatriated** to distant lands such as North Korea or China. While they may look Korean or Chinese, they do not speak the languages and have not had ties with these parts of the world for many years. As the newly formed republics try to **reinvigorate** their traditions and values, many of the ethnic minorities tend to feel left out with no place to really call home.

5   The fall of the Soviet Union is perhaps one of the most **momentous** events of the twentieth century. Walls fell, markets opened, and people rejoiced in the streets, anticipating a life full of opportunities and freedom to make their own choices. A system that took so long to build will probably need as much time, if not more, to truly adapt to the free enterprise system that is now the world model.

a shift: a change
subsidize: to finance, support
a fluctuation: a movement or change
sovereignty: self-government, supremacy
forefront: in the position of most
    importance, vanguard

repatriate: to send people back to their
    original homeland
reinvigorate: to revitalize, bring back to life
momentous: important, eventful

3. What is the writer's main message in this essay?

   _____

   _____

4. Reread the thesis statement of "The Fall." Is the thesis stated or implied?

   _____

5. In Paragraph 2, the writer explains that one effect of the Soviet breakup is the new market economy. What examples does the writer give to show that countries are now in a market economy?

   _____

   _____

6. In Paragraph 4, the author writes about ethnic minorities and their problems. Which minorities are specifically mentioned and what problems are they having?

   _____

   _____

7. In Paragraph 2, find a word that has approximately the same meaning as the word *shift* and write it

   here. _____

8. Find the boldfaced vocabulary word in the final paragraph of this essay. Write a synonym of that

   word here. _____

🔨 Building Better Sentences

Correct and varied sentence structure is essential to the quality of your writing. For further practice with "The Fall," go to Practice 16 on page 177 in Appendix 1.

Developing Cause-Effect Essays

In this next section, you will work on cause-effect essays as you make an outline, write supporting information, study connectors, and choose a topic. Practicing these skills will help you write an effective cause-effect essay.

Complete the following two outlines with a partner. The first one outlines the causes of bullying behavior (focus-on-causes method), and the second one outlines the effects of bullying on the young people who are being bullied (focus-on-effects method). Use your imagination, knowledge of the topic, and understanding of essay organization. (See Unit 1 for a review of the structure of an essay.) Be sure to pay attention to the thesis statements and use them to help you complete the outlines.

Focus-on-Causes Outline

Topic: The causes of bullying behavior

I. Introduction (Paragraph 1)

    A. Hook: _____

        _____

    B. Thesis statement: Bullying behavior can occur for many reasons, some of which are _____

        _____

        _____

        _____

II. Body

    A. Paragraph 2 (Cause 1) topic sentence: Teens often begin bullying because they want to control those who are weaker than they are.

        1. Bullying gives young people an identity—they become well-known in school.

        2. Bullying makes them feel powerful.

        3. _____

SUPPORT

B. Paragraph 3 (Cause 2) topic sentence: _____

_____

    1. In many families, both parents work outside the home.

    2. Parents often do not have time to pay attention to their children's needs.

    3. Parents may not be aware of the aggressive behavior that their children are exhibiting, either inside or outside the home.

C. Paragraph 4 (Cause 3) topic sentence: _____

_____

    1. They use violence as a way of identifying themselves.

    2. They may have emotional problems.

    3. Being known for bad behavior is better than not being known at all.

III. Conclusion (Paragraph 5) (restated thesis): _____

_____

_____

_____

The best way to stop young people from bullying and abusing their peers is to educate the public—including teachers, parents, and other children—that bullying is an absolutely unacceptable behavior. Only then will there be a decrease in the number of bullying incidents in school.

Focus-on-Effects Outline

Topic: The effects of bullying on the victim

  I. Introduction (Paragraph 1)

    A. Hook: _____

_____

_____

    B. Thesis statement: When young people bully others, the effects felt by the weaker student can lead to serious, even deadly, consequences.

  II. Body

    A. Paragraph 2 (Effect 1) topic sentence: Students who are bullied tend to withdraw from society.

      1. They often stop communicating with parents and friends.

      2. They want to hide this embarrassing situation, which can lead to lying.

      3. _____

    B. Paragraph 3 (Effect 2) topic sentence: _____

_____

_____

      1. Students lose self-esteem and start questioning their own personalities, thinking that maybe they deserve this bad treatment.

      2. They may start focusing only on the bully.

      3. Their outlook on life may become darker and darker as the bullying continues.

C. Paragraph 4 (Effect 3) topic sentence: If teens become damaged by the bullying, they may do almost anything to get out of the situation.

   1. They may try to escape from their painful reality by engaging in dangerous activities.

   2. They might think about a plan of revenge.

   3. _____

III. Conclusion (Paragraph 5) (restated thesis): _____

_____

When young people are victims of bullies, there is a strong chance that they will suffer many negative consequences, not only from the bullies themselves but also as they begin to separate from society. For so many years, bullying was considered a normal part of growing up, as in the saying "Boys will be boys!" However, with the increase of teen anguish due to bullying and the millions of dollars spent on long-term therapy, one has to wonder if bullying should be considered a "normal" activity. In order to ensure a stable and healthy society, individuals need to take a harder look at this negative behavior that hurts not only the bullied child and the bully, but the family and society as a whole.

ACTIVITY 4 Supporting Information

The following cause-effect essay is missing the supporting information. As you read the essay, work with a partner to write supporting sentences for each paragraph. If you need more space, use a separate piece of paper. After you finish, compare your supporting information with that of other students.

Did you watch TV when you were a child? In this essay, you provide some facts about children and TV watching.

Television at Its Worst

1   Mr. Stevenson has just come home from a terribly tiring day at work. The first thing he does, after taking off his tie and shoes, is plop down on the couch and turn on the television. Does this sound like a normal routine? It should because Mr. Stevenson's actions are repeated by millions around the world. People use television to relax and to forget about their daily troubles. However, what started out decades ago as an exciting, new type of family entertainment is currently being blamed for problems, especially in children. Many researchers now claim that too much television is not good for kids. They have a point; watching too much TV often does have negative effects on youngsters.

2   One negative effect of TV on kids is laziness. _____
_____
_____
_____
_____

3   Another problem with TV watching and kids is that children may have difficulty distinguishing between what is real and what is not. _____
_____
_____
_____
_____
_____

4   Finally, television may lead children to _____.
_____
_____
_____
_____
_____

5   Television has changed over the years to include more and more programs that are inappropriate for children. For TV to once again play a more positive role in children's lives, something must be done. Young people's futures depend on it.

Building Better Sentences

Correct and varied sentence structure is essential to the quality of your writing. For further practice with "Television at Its Worst," go to Practice 17 on page 178 in Appendix 1.

Writer's Note

Sequencing Paragraphs

Some writers like to present their strongest or most forceful information in the first or second paragraphs of an essay. Other writers prefer to end their essays with the strongest information. Both ways are correct. Choose the sequence of paragraphs that best presents your information in the way that you want your reader to understand it.

Language Focus

Connectors for Cause-Effect Essays

Connectors show relationships between ideas in sentences and paragraphs. In cause-effect essays, writers commonly use the connecting words and phrases in the following charts. (For a more complete list of connectors, see the Brief Writer's Handbook with Activities, pages 156–157.)

Connectors That Show Cause	
On account of As a result of Because of Due to	the rain, we all got wet.
Because Since	it rained, we all got wet.

Connectors That Show Effect		
It rained.	For this reason, Therefore, As a result, Thus, Consequently,	we all got wet.

Read the next student essay (focus-on-effects method) and circle the appropriate connector in each set of parentheses. Refer to the list in the Language Focus section on page 95, if necessary.

Do you use computers in your academic work? Read about how computers have made academic work easier.

Effects of Computers on Higher Education

1   Through the ages, industrious individuals have continuously created conveniences to make life easier. From the invention of the wheel to the lightbulb, inventions have propelled society forward. One recent modern invention is the computer, which has improved many aspects of people's lives. This is especially true in the field of education. (Therefore / Because of) computer technology, higher education today has three major conveniences: lecture variety, easy research, and time-saving writing methods.

2   One important effect of computer technology on higher education is the **availability** of lectures. (For this reason / As a result of) the development of computer networks, students can obtain lectures from many universities in real time. They are now able to sit down in front of a digital screen and listen to a lecture being given at another university. In addition, **interactive** media can be used to question a lecturer or exchange opinions with other students **via** e-mail. Such computerized lectures give students **access** to knowledge that was previously unavailable. (For this reason / Because), students can learn from professors in specialized fields, regardless of where they are teaching.

availability: accessibility, ease of use
interactive: involving more than one person

via: through the use of
access: contact with, right to use

3   The development of computers also makes it possible to have access to more information via the Internet and databases. (Since / Consequently), when students research a topic, they do not necessarily have to go to the library to find information because many articles and even textbooks can be downloaded via computer. It is now extremely easy to use the Internet and databases since all one has to do is type in a few key words and wait a few moments. The convenience of doing this type of research from home helps busy students who would otherwise not have time to visit a campus library.

4   Finally, computer technology helps students with their academic writing assignments. E-mail assignments are becoming more common at universities. (As a result / Due to), the assignments are much quicker and easier to finish than before. When it is time to hand in assigned papers or homework, students simply send them to their professors via e-mail. This method is beneficial for students and convenient for teachers, who will not risk losing their students' work in a mountain of papers. Another time-saving computer function is the word processor. (Thus / Because of) improved word-processing programs, students have the added benefit of spell-checking and grammar-checking programs. If a sentence is grammatically incorrect, one of these programs highlights the incorrect parts of the sentence and corrects them. Word-processing programs also have built-in dictionaries and spell checkers, which help students write concisely and accurately. (Since / As a result of) these two functions—e-mail and word processing—both teachers and students can save a great deal of time and produce solid work.

5   To summarize, computer technology has three main positive effects on higher education: lecture variety, easy research, and time-saving writing methods. (Because of / Because) the **advent** of computers in education, students can now increase their knowledge and be more time-efficient at the same time. Academic life will never be the same!

the advent: the beginning

 For more practice with connectors that show cause and effect, try Unit 4, Activity 2 and Activity 3 on the *Great Writing 4* Web site: elt.heinle.com/greatwriting

⚒ Building Better Sentences

Correct and varied sentence structure is essential to the quality of your writing. For further practice with "Effects of Computers on Higher Education," go to Practice 18 on page 179 in Appendix 1.

Choosing Words Carefully

In all writing, including cause-effect essays, attention to precise language is important. Wordiness, or using unnecessary words, is a common problem for many writers. If you can eliminate wordiness from your writing, your essays will be clearer and easier to read.

Wordiness

Some writers think that the more words they use, the better their essay will sound. However, in academic writing in English, it is important to be as concise as possible. Unnecessary words and phrases do not improve your writing. Instead, they make it hard for readers to understand what you want to say.

The list on the left contains common wordy phrases. Try to avoid them in your writing.

Change	To
it goes without saying	(nothing)
at that point in time	at that time
despite the fact that + subject + verb	despite + noun
for all intents and purposes	(nothing)
in the vicinity of	near
in the final analysis	finally
made a statement saying	said
in the event that	if
the reason why is	because
it seems unnecessary to point out	(nothing)
when all is said and done	(nothing)

ACTIVITY 6 Wordiness

The following introductory paragraph from a cause-effect essay contains 6 examples of wordy phrases. Underline them as you find them. Then, on a separate piece of paper, rewrite the paragraph without the wordy phrases and make it more concise. Note: There is more than one correct way of rewriting this paragraph.

EXAMPLE PARAGRAPH

The fat-free food industry is a tremendous money-making business although recent research has shown that fat-free products are considered only a minor prescription for the purpose of losing weight. Nutritionists have made statements saying that, for all intents and purposes, more important steps to losing weight are exercising and eating well-balanced meals. Despite the fact that this information has appeared, many people still seem to believe that, when all is said and done, eating fat-free food is the best dieting method. The contents of the following essay show some interesting reasons for this fat-free phenomenon.

Redundancy

Redundancy—a kind of wordiness—is the unnecessary repetition of information. When you write, you may want to impress your readers with an eloquent essay that is full of thought-provoking information. One way that writers often try to do this is by loading up on information. You may think, "The more information I have in my essay, the more my readers will enjoy it." This is not usually the case, especially if, instead of adding information, you repeat what you have already said. Repetition can occur in the wording of short phrases as well as in sentences.

Redundant phrases   The list on the left contains commonly used redundant phrases. Try to avoid them in your writing. (If you are not sure why the phrases are redundant, look up the meanings of the two words.)

Change	To
collaborate together	collaborate
completely unanimous	unanimous
courthouse building	courthouse
descend downward	descend
erupt violently	erupt
exactly identical	identical
free gift	gift
merge together	merge
repeat again	repeat
unexpected surprise	surprise

Redundant sentences   The second sentence below contains the same information as the first sentence.

> The United States is the most influential power in the world. Partly because of its abundant material resources and stable political system, this country has great influence in global affairs.

Combine the sentences and eliminate the redundant information. Read the combined sentence below.

> The United States has a great influence in global affairs in part because of its abundant material resources and stable political system.

 For practice with identifying redundant phrases, try Unit 4, Activity 4 on the *Great Writing 4* Web site: elt.heinle.com/greatwriting

Underline the redundant information in this paragraph. Then compare your work with a partner's.

Many people love to watch science-fiction stories on TV or at the movies. TV shows and films, such as *Star Trek*, are popular not only because they creatively show how future life might be in three hundred years, but also because they introduce us to characters from other worlds, planets, and galaxies. Perhaps one of the most popular kinds of characters in these futuristic programs is a person with ESP, or extrasensory perception. ESP is a sense that allows one person to read the mind of another without the exchange of words. These characters, who can read minds and know the innermost thoughts and secrets of other people, often use their gift in less than noble ways. One must remember, however, that these scenes take place in an untrue and fictitious situation. A more interesting concept is to think about what would really happen if ordinary, everyday people possessed ESP.

For more practice with identifying redundant sentences in a paragraph, try Unit 4, Activity 5 and Activity 6 on the *Great Writing 4* Web site: elt.heinle.com/greatwriting

ACTIVITY 8 Word Associations

Circle the word or phrase that is most closely related to the word or phrase on the left. If necessary, use a dictionary to check the meaning of words you do not know.

1. via	using		far away
2. an ideology	beliefs		smart
3. momentous	boring		important
4. interactive	not alone		alone
5. the advent	termination		beginning
6. to rejoice	sad feelings		happy feelings
7. the forefront	new ideas		old ideas
8. availability	presence		thought
9. to propel	to move forward		to stay in one place
10. a blunder	a mistake		an opinion

ACTIVITY 9 Using Collocations

Fill in each blank with the word or phrase on the left that most naturally completes the phrase on the right. If necessary, use a dictionary to check the meaning of words you do not know.

1. time / lunch   to have a difficult _____

2. on / to   one negative effect of TV _____ people

3. up to / out of   to get _____ a bad situation

4. by / for   convenient _____ everyone

5. excited / added   an _____ benefit

6. play / run   to _____ a role

7. give / do   to _____ access to something

8. part / step   a normal _____ of life

9. for / to   to resort _____ an alternative plan

10. in / to   children tend _____ be active

Developing Ideas for Writing

Good writers work with ideas that will interest readers. How do writers come up with good ideas? This section will show you some ways to generate ideas for cause-effect essays.

✎ Writer's Note

Asking Questions

Many writers can think of good topics, but they have trouble developing their topics into essays. One brainstorming method that often helps is to ask questions about the topic—*Who? What? Where? When? Why? How?* This process often leads to new ideas that can be used in an essay. Especially for a cause-effect essay, good writers ask the question *Why?* This analytical question will exercise your skills in finding cause-effect relationships.

ACTIVITY 10 Starting with Questions

The following questions can all be developed into cause-effect essays. Try to give at least three answers to each question.

1. Why do people gain too much weight?

   _____

   _____

   _____

2. What usually happens after a stock market crash?

   _____

   _____

   _____

3. Why do airplane crashes occur?

   _____

   _____

   _____

4. What would happen if society used a barter system instead of money?

_____

_____

_____

5. Why are more and more people studying a second (or third) language?

_____

_____

_____

6. What are the effects of playing a team sport?

_____

_____

_____

7. What are the causes of _____? (Think of your own topic.)

_____

_____

_____

8. What are the effects of _____? (Think of your own topic.)

_____

_____

_____

For more practice with using questions to develop ideas for topics, try Unit 4, Activity 7 on the *Great Writing 4* Web site: elt.heinle.com/greatwriting

🌩 Brainstorming

In the next activity, you will use a brainstorming technique called **clustering**. (See Unit 2 for a review of this technique.) Here is an example of clustering; the topic is the effects of ozone depletion on the environment.

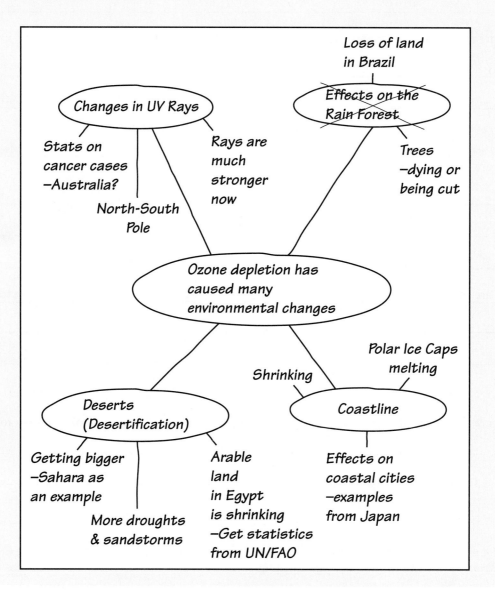

Original Student Writing: Cause-Effect Essay

ACTIVITY 11 Clustering Ideas

Choose a topic from Activity 10. With the preceding example as a guide, brainstorm some ideas about your topic using the clustering method. Write all your ideas. When you have finished, cross out the ideas that you do not like or do not want to include in your essay. Explain your brainstorming cluster to a classmate.

Complete the outline below as a guide to help you brainstorm a more detailed plan for your cause-effect essay. Use your ideas from Activity 11. You may need to use either more or fewer points under each heading. Write in complete sentences where possible.

Topic: _____

   I. Introduction (Paragraph 1)

      A. Hook: _____

      B. Connecting information: _____

          _____

      C. Thesis statement: _____

          _____

  II. Body

      A. Paragraph 2 (first cause or effect) topic sentence: _____

          _____

          1. _____

          2. _____

          3. _____

      B. Paragraph 3 (second cause or effect) topic sentence: _____

          _____

          1. _____

          2. _____

          3. _____

      C. Paragraph 4 (third cause or effect) topic sentence: _____

          _____

          1. _____

          2. _____

          3. _____

 III. Conclusion (paragraph 5)

      A. Restated thesis: _____

          _____

      B. Suggestion, opinion, or prediction: _____

          _____

SUPPORT

SUPPORT

SUPPORT

Personal Writing Style

Some writers work well from an outline and some do not. Some writers write the introduction first, and some write it last. Writing is an individual activity. Use the guidelines in this book and follow the process that works best for you.

ACTIVITY 13 Peer Editing Your Outline

Exchange books with a partner and look at Activity 12. Read your partner's outline. Then use Peer Editing Sheet 5 on page 193 to help you comment on your partner's outline. Use your partner's feedback to revise your outline. Make sure you have enough information to develop your supporting sentences.

ACTIVITY 14 Writing a Cause-Effect Essay

Write a cause-effect essay based on your revised outline from Activity 13. Use at least five of the vocabulary words or phrases presented in Activity 8 and Activity 9. Underline these words and phrases in your essay. Be sure to refer to the seven steps in the writing process in the Brief Writer's Handbook with Activities on pages 131–138.

ACTIVITY 15 Peer Editing Your Essay

Exchange papers from Activity 14 with a partner. Read your partner's writing. Then use Peer Editing Sheet 6 on page 195 to help you comment on your partner's writing. Be sure to offer positive suggestions and comments that will help your partner improve his or her writing. Consider your partner's comments as you revise your own writing.

Additional Topics for Writing

Here are more ideas for topics for a cause-effect essay. Before you write, be sure to refer to the seven steps in the writing process in the Brief Writer's Handbook with Activities, pages 131–138.

TOPIC 1:   Children are learning to use computers at a very early age. What are some effects (positive or negative) that computers can have on the intellectual development of children?

TOPIC 2:   Going to college is a dream for many people. Some do the work, graduate, and find good jobs. Other students, however, never finish their university studies. Write an essay about what causes students to drop out of college.

TOPIC 3:   Friendships are an integral part of a person's life. Unfortunately, some of these relationships do not last. Write an essay highlighting some of the reasons that friendships sometimes die.

TOPIC 4:   The number of car accidents that occur on a daily basis is massive. In your opinion, what are three common causes of motor vehicle accidents?

TOPIC 5:   Many people enjoy traveling and experiencing other cultures. What are some of the beneficial effects of international travel on an individual?

Timed Writing

How quickly can you write in English? There are many times when you must write quickly, such as on a test. It is important to feel comfortable during those times. Timed-writing practice can make you feel better about writing quickly in English.

First, read the essay guidelines below. Then take out a piece of paper. Read the writing prompt below the guidelines. As quickly as you can, write a basic outline for this writing prompt (including the thesis and your three main points). You should spend <u>no more than</u> 5 minutes on your outline.

You will then have 40 minutes to write a 5-paragraph cause-effect essay about your topic. At the end of the 40 minutes, your teacher will collect your work and return it to you at a later date.

Cause-Effect Essay Guidelines

- Use the focus-on-causes method.

- Remember to give your essay a title.

- Double-space your essay.

- Write as legibly as possible (if you are not using a computer).

- Include a short introduction (with a thesis statement), three body paragraphs, and a conclusion.

- Try to give yourself a few minutes before the end of the activity to review your work. Check for spelling, verb tense, and subject-verb agreement mistakes.

> Why do people keep pets?

Argumentative Essays

GOAL: To learn how to write an argumentative essay

*Language Focus: Controlling tone with modals

What Is an Argumentative Essay?

In an **argumentative essay**, the writer's purpose is to persuade the audience to agree with his or her opinion about a controversial topic. In a sociology class, for example, you might write an essay arguing that female military personnel can be as effective as male military personnel in combat missions. In a history class, your essay might try to convince readers that World War I could have been avoided if certain steps had been taken. In an argumentative essay, sometimes referred

to as a **persuasive essay**, the writer states his or her opinion, gives reasons to support it, and tries to convince the audience that he or she is right.

Arguing Pro or Con

Choosing a topic that is appropriate for an argumentative essay is especially important because some things cannot be argued. For example, you cannot argue that a rose is more beautiful than a daisy—this is an opinion that cannot be supported by facts. However, you can argue that roses are more popular than daisies and support the argument with facts about florists' sales of the two kinds of flowers.

Here are a few effective topics and thesis statements for an argumentative essay:

- Marriage before the age of eighteen: People under the age of eighteen should not be allowed to marry.

- Standardized testing: Standardized testing should not be required as part of the application process for a university.

- Fast-food restaurants: Communities should decide if fast-food restaurants are right for their neighborhood.

You can argue either for (**pro**) or against (**con**) these statements. If your topic does not have two viewpoints, your essay will not be effective. Look at the following example of an ineffective topic and thesis statement.

Jazz music: Jazz music began with African-Americans.

You cannot argue against this statement because it is a fact. Therefore, you cannot write an argumentative essay using this thesis statement.

Writer's Note

Choosing a Topic

Be sure that the topic you choose for an argumentative essay has two sides. In other words, your topic should have a pro argument and a con argument.

 For practice with thesis statements for argumentative essays, try Unit 5, Activity 1 on the *Great Writing 4* Web site: elt.heinle.com/greatwriting

Convincing the Reader

Your job as the writer of an argumentative essay is to convince your readers that your opinion about a topic (your thesis statement) is the most valid viewpoint. To do this, your essay needs to be balanced—it must include an opposing viewpoint, or **counterargument** (see page 113). Even though you are arguing one side of an issue (either for or against), you must think about what someone on the other side of the issue would argue. As soon as you give your opponent's point of view, you must offer a **refutation** of it (see page 113). This means that you refute the other point of view, or show how it is wrong. If you give only your opinion, your essay will sound like propaganda, and your readers will not be convinced of your viewpoint.

Example Argumentative Essay

A good way to help you learn how to write an argumentative essay is to study an example. In the next activity, you will read and study the content and organization of an example essay.

ACTIVITY 1   Studying an Example Essay

Discuss the questions that come before the example essay with a partner. Then read the essay. Work with a partner to answer the questions after the essay.

In this essay, the writer argues for the use of school uniforms.

1. Did you wear a uniform when you went to school?

2. Some people believe that children are too materialistic these days. For example, they may be too interested in wearing brand-name clothes and shoes. What is your opinion?

EXAMPLE ESSAY 19

The School Uniform Question

1   Individualism is a **fundamental** part of society in many countries. Most people believe in the right to express their own opinion without fear of punishment. This value, however, is coming under fire in an unlikely place—the **public school** classroom. The issue is school uniforms. Should public school students be allowed to make individual decisions about clothing, or should all students be required to wear a uniform? School uniforms are the better choice for three reasons.

fundamental: essential, basic

a public school: a school run by the state government and paid for by citizens' property taxes

2 First, wearing school uniforms would help make students' lives simpler. They would no longer have to decide what to wear every morning, sometimes trying on outfit after outfit in an effort to choose. Uniforms would not only save time but also would eliminate the stress often associated with this chore.

3 Second, school uniforms influence students to act responsibly in groups and as individuals. Uniforms give students the message that school is a special place for learning. In addition, uniforms create a feeling of unity among students. For example, when students do something as a group, such as attend meetings in the auditorium or eat lunch in the cafeteria, the fact that they all wear the same uniform gives them a sense of community. Even more important, statistics show the positive effects that school uniforms have on violence and **truancy**. According to a recent survey in a large school district in Florida, incidents of school violence dropped by 50 percent, attendance and test scores improved, and student suspensions declined approximately 30 percent after school uniforms were introduced.

4 Finally, school uniforms would help make all the students feel equal. Students' standards of living differ greatly from family to family, and some people are **well-off** while others are not. People sometimes forget that school is a place to get an education, not to promote a "fashion show." **Implementing** mandatory school uniforms would make all the students look the same regardless of their financial status. School uniforms would promote pride and help to raise the self-esteem of students who cannot afford to wear expensive clothing.

5 Opponents of mandatory uniforms say that students who wear school uniforms cannot express their individuality. This point has some merit on the surface. However, as stated previously, school is a place to learn, not to **flaunt** wealth and fashion. Society must decide if individual expression through clothing is more valuable than improved educational performance. It is important to remember that school uniforms would be worn only during school hours. Students can express their individuality in the way that they dress outside of the classroom.

6 In conclusion, there are many well-documented benefits of implementing mandatory school uniforms for students. Studies show that students learn better and act more responsibly when they wear uniforms. Public schools should require uniforms in order to benefit both the students and society as a whole.

truancy: absence without permission
well-off: wealthy
implement: to put into effect
flaunt: to show off, display

3. The topic of this essay is school uniforms. What is the hook in the first paragraph?

_____

_____

4. What is the thesis statement? _____

_____

_____

5. Paragraphs 2, 3, and 4 each give a reason for requiring school uniforms. These reasons can be found in the topic sentence of each paragraph. What are the reasons?

Paragraph 2: _____

_____

Paragraph 3: _____

_____

Paragraph 4: _____

_____

6. In Paragraph 4, what supporting information does the writer give to show that uniforms make students equal?

_____

_____

_____

7. Which paragraph presents a counterargument—an argument that is contrary to, or the opposite of, the writer's opinion? _____ What is the counterargument?

_____

_____

_____

8. The writer gives a refutation of the counterargument by showing that it is invalid. What is the writer's refutation?

_____

_____

_____

9. Write the sentence from the concluding paragraph that restates the thesis.

_____

_____

_____

10. Reread the concluding paragraph. What is the writer's opinion about this issue?

_____

_____

_____

Correct and varied sentence structure is essential to the quality of your writing. For further practice with "The School Uniform Question," go to Practice 19 on page 180 in Appendix 1.

Counterargument and Refutation

The key technique to persuading the reader that your viewpoint is valid is to support it in every paragraph. While this is not a problem in the first few paragraphs of your essay, the **counterargument** goes against your thesis statement. Consequently, every counterargument that you include in your essay needs a refutation. A **refutation** is a response to the counterargument that disproves it.

Look at the following excerpts from two argumentative essays in this unit. The counterarguments are in *italics* and the refutations are underlined.

From Example Essay 19:

Opponents of mandatory uniforms say that students who wear school uniforms cannot express their individuality. This point has some merit on the surface. However, as stated previously, school is a place to learn, not to flaunt wealth and fashion.

From Essay in Activity 2:

Some parents might disagree and claim that only academic subjects should be taught in school. Then again, most parents do not have the time or the resources to see to it that their children are getting enough exercise.

As you can see, what begins as a counterargument ends up as another reason in support of your opinion.

For practice with identifying counterarguments and refutations, try Unit 5, Activity 2 and Activity 3 on the *Great Writing 4* Web site: elt.heinle.com/greatwriting

Writer's Note

Arguing Your Point of View

Imagine that you are having an argument with a friend about your topic. She disagrees with your opinion. What do you think will be her strongest argument against your point of view? How will you respond to this counterargument? (Your answer is your refutation.)

Developing Argumentative Essays

In this next section, you will work on argumentative essays as you make an outline, write supporting information, study modals, and choose a topic.

Outlining

ACTIVITY 2 Outlining Practice

The following outline, which is designed for an argumentative essay, is missing some supporting information. Work with a partner to complete the outline. Use your imagination, knowledge of the topic, and understanding of essay organization to complete this outline with your partner. After you finish, compare your supporting information with other students' work.

Topic: Mandatory physical education in school

I. Introduction (Paragraph 1)

    Thesis statement: Physical education classes should be required for all public school students in all grades.

II. Body

    A. Paragraph 2 (Pro argument 1) topic sentence: Physical education courses promote children's general health.

        1. Researchers have proved that exercise has maximum benefit if done regularly.

        2. _____

        3. Students should learn the importance of physical fitness at an early age.

B. Paragraph 3 (Pro argument 2) topic sentence: Physical education teaches children transferable life skills.

    1. Kids learn about teamwork while playing team sports.

    2. Kids learn about the benefits of healthy competition.

    3. _____

C. Paragraph 4 (Pro argument 3) topic sentence: _____

_____

    1. Trained physical education teachers can teach more effectively than parents.

    2. Physical education teachers can usually point students toward new and interesting sports.

    3. Schools generally have the appropriate facilities and equipment.

D. Paragraph 5 (counterargument and refutation)

    1. Counterargument: Some parents might disagree and claim that only academic subjects should be taught in school.

    2. Refutation: Then again, most parents do not have the time or the resources to see to it that their children are getting enough exercise.

III. Conclusion (Paragraph 6) (restated thesis): _____

_____

Physical education has often been downplayed as a minor part of daily school life. If its benefits are taken into account and if schools adopt a twelve-year fitness plan, the positive results will foster a new awareness of not only physical fitness but also communication skills.

Adding Supporting Information

ACTIVITY 3 Studying the Supporting Information in an Example Essay

Discuss the questions that come before the essay with a partner. Then read the essay. You will find that this argumentative essay is missing the supporting information. As you read the essay, work with a partner to write supporting sentences for each paragraph. If you need more space, use a separate piece of paper. After you finish, compare your supporting information with that of other students.

In this essay, the writer argues against gun ownership.

1. Do you know anyone who owns a gun? Why does that person have a gun?

2. Have you ever shot a gun? If so, describe the circumstances when you did this. Why did you shoot a gun? Where were you? When was this?

Sidebar labels: SUPPORT (×3)

No More Guns

1   The year 1774 was **pivotal** in the history of the United States. It marked the beginning of the Revolutionary War, which lasted 13 years and claimed thousands of lives. Fighting against the British, the Americans had to rely on individual citizens because they did not have a well-organized army. As farmers and hunters, many citizens already owned guns. These rifles proved **indispensable** in defeating the British. After
the war, citizens were **reluctant** to **give up** their rifles as they feared future invasions. Because of this fear, an **amendment** was added to the Constitution of the United States guaranteeing citizens the right to bear arms. Times have changed, however. The United States has one of the largest military forces in the world, and Americans are no longer called upon to use their own weapons in the military. Although people no longer need guns for this purpose, there are in fact over 200,000,000 guns in circulation. Unfortunately, gun-related deaths continue to increase every year, with many innocent people losing their lives. Despite the original intention of the Second Amendment, the United States would be much better off if ownership of guns by private citizens was **outlawed**.

2   The first benefit of making guns illegal is that the number of accidental shootings would decrease.

_____

_____

_____

_____

3   Another benefit of outlawing guns is that the streets would be safer.

_____

_____

_____

_____

pivotal: key, essential
indispensable: necessary, essential
reluctant: unwilling

give up: to surrender, agree not to own
an amendment: a modification, change
outlaw: to ban, forbid

4   If guns were illegal, people would be less likely to harm loved ones in moments of anger.

_____

_____

_____

_____

5   Some people say that they feel safer having a gun at home. However, if guns were more difficult to own, fewer criminals would have them. Fewer guns would lead to a decrease in the number of gun-related crimes and victims.

_____

_____

_____

_____

6   Statistics show that the occurrence of violent crime is much lower in countries that do not allow citizens to carry weapons. Although it is doubtful that the United States would ever completely outlaw the private ownership of weapons, how nice it would be to lower the risk of being shot. It is time for the United States to take a close look at its **antiquated** gun laws and make some changes for the safety of its citizens.

antiquated: out of date, old-fashioned

Building Better Sentences

Correct and varied sentence structure is essential to the quality of your writing. For further practice with "No More Guns," go to Practice 20 on page 181 in Appendix 1.

Writer's Note

Modals and Tone

Modals can change the tone of a sentence. Modals such as _must_ and _had better_ make a verb stronger. Other modals such as _may, might, should, can_, and _could_ make a verb softer. Remember to use modals to strengthen or soften your verbs. For example, "The president must change his policy" is very strong, but "The president should change his policy" is softer.

Language Focus

Controlling Tone with Modals

In argumentative essays, good writers are aware of how their arguments sound. Are they too strong? Not strong enough? Certain words can help control the tone of your argument.

Asserting a Point

Strong modals such as *must* and *had better* help writers to assert their main points. When you use these words, readers know where you stand on an issue.

Examples:

The facts clearly show that researchers <u>must</u> stop unethical animal testing.

People who value their health <u>had better</u> stop smoking now.

Acknowledging an Opposing Point

Weaker modals such as *may, might, could, can,* and *would* help writers make an opposing opinion sound weak. You acknowledge an opposing point when you use *may*, for example, but this weak modal shows that the statement is not strong and can be refuted more easily.

Examples:

While it <u>may</u> be true that people have eaten meat for a long time, the number one killer of Americans now is heart disease, caused in part by the consumption of large amounts of animal fat.

Some citizens <u>may</u> be against mandatory military service, but those who do serve in the military often have a strong sense of pride and personal satisfaction.

Writer's Note

Using Modals for Assertion and for Acknowledging an Opposing View

You are probably already familiar with most of the modals in English—*may, might, can, could, would, must, should, had better,* and *ought to*. Modals can be useful in argumentative essays for two reasons—strong modals help writers make their opinions sound stronger, and weak modals make opposing views sound weaker.

Read the following argumentative essay. Circle the modal in parentheses that you feel is more appropriate.

Life or Death?

1   How would you feel if a loved one were murdered? Would you want retribution, or would sending the killer to prison be enough? This question has been asked many times, but people are not in agreement about the ultimate punishment. We all know that it is wrong to take a human life, but if our government does the killing, is it still a crime? Some people say that the government does not have the right to end someone's life, but the following reasons (might / will) show why capital punishment should be preserved.

2   The first reason for allowing the death penalty is for the sake of punishment itself. Most people agree that criminals who commit serious crimes (might / should) be separated from society. The punishment (will / ought to) depend on the degree of the crime. Capital punishment, the most severe form of punishment, ends criminals' lives. It seems reasonable that this severe punishment be reserved for those who commit the most serious of crimes.

3   The second reason to preserve capital punishment is financial. The government (should / will) not have to spend a lot of money on criminals. Next to capital punishment, the most severe punishment is a life sentence in prison, where the government (might / has to) take care of criminals until they die naturally. These criminals do not work, but they receive free housing and food. It is unfair to use tax dollars for such a purpose.

4   The last reason for continuing the use of the death penalty is based on the purpose of government. If the government has legitimate power to make, judge, and carry out the laws, it (may / should) also have the power to decide if criminals should die. Capital punishment is like any other sentence. If one believes that the government has the right to charge a fine or put criminals into jail, then the government (could / must) also have the same power to decide the fate of a prisoner's life.

5 The opponents of capital punishment (must / might) say that nobody has the right to decide who should die, including the government. However, when the government sends soldiers into war, in some way, it is deciding those soldiers' fate; some will live and some will be killed. As long as the government has the right to send its citizens to the battlefield, it has a right to put criminals to death.

6 There are many good reasons to preserve capital punishment. Certainly not every criminal (can / should) be put to death. Capital punishment (ought to / will) be viewed as the harshest form of punishment. If no punishment (can / should) reform a murderer, then capital punishment is the best thing that can be done for that person and for society.

 For more practice with controlling tone with modals, try Unit 5, Activity 4 on the *Great Writing 4* Web site: elt.heinle.com/greatwriting

🔨 Building Better Sentences

Correct and varied sentence structure is essential to the quality of your writing. For further practice with "Life or Death?," go to Practice 21 on page 182 in Appendix 1.

Choosing a Topic

ACTIVITY 5 Writing Pro and Con Thesis Statements

Read the following list of topics for argumentative essays. For each topic, write a pro (for) thesis statement and a con (against) thesis statement related to the topic. Then compare your statements with your classmates' statements. The first one has been done for you.

1. Topic: Women in the military

   Pro thesis statement: <u>In a society where women are chief executive officers of companies, leaders of nations, and family breadwinners, there is no reason why they should not play an active role in the military.</u>

   Con thesis statement: <u>Women should not be allowed to fight in the military because they do not have the strength or endurance required in combat.</u>

2. Topic: Using animals in disease research

Pro thesis statement: _____

_____

Con thesis statement: _____

_____

3. Topic: Driver's license age restrictions

Pro thesis statement: _____

_____

Con thesis statement: _____

_____

4. Topic: Space exploration

Pro thesis statement: _____

_____

Con thesis statement: _____

_____

5. Topic: Internet privacy

Pro thesis statement: _____

_____

Con thesis statement: _____

_____

For more practice with pro and con thesis statements, try Unit 5, Activity 5 on the *Great Writing 4* Web site: elt.heinle.com/greatwriting

Avoiding Faulty Logic

Good writers want to convince readers to agree with their arguments—their reasons and conclusions. If your arguments are not logical, you will not persuade your readers. Logic can help prove your point and disprove your opponent's point—and perhaps change your reader's mind about an issue. If you use faulty logic (logic not based on fact), readers will not believe you or take your position seriously.

This section presents a few logical errors that writers sometimes make in argumentative essays. Try to avoid these errors in your writing.

Sweeping Generalizations

Words such as *all*, *always*, and *never* are too broad and cannot be supported.

Example:	All Americans eat fast food.
Problem:	Maybe every American that you know eats fast food, but the statement that all Americans eat it cannot be proven.

Events Related Only by Sequence

When one event happens, it does not necessarily cause a second event to happen, even if one follows the other in time.

Example:	Henry went to the football game, and then he had a car accident. Therefore, football games cause car accidents.
Problem:	The two events may have happened in that order, but do not mislead the reader into thinking that the first action was responsible for the second.

Inappropriate Authority Figures

Using famous names may often help you prove or disprove your point. However, be sure to use the name logically and in the proper context.

Example:	Madonna is a good singer. As a result, she would make a good orchestra conductor.
Problem:	While Madonna may be a good singer, this quality will not necessarily make her a good orchestra conductor.

Hasty Generalizations

Hasty generalizations are just what they sound like—making quick judgments based on inadequate information. This kind of logical fallacy is a common error in argumentative writing.

Example:	Joe did not want to study at a university. Instead, he decided to go to a technical school. He is now making an excellent salary repairing computers. Bill does not want to study at a university. Therefore, he should go to a technical school to become financially successful.
Problem:	While Joe and Bill have something in common (they do not want to study at a university), this fact alone does not mean that Bill would be successful doing the same thing that Joe has done. Other information may be important as well, such as the fact that Joe has lots of experience with computers or that Bill has problems with manual dexterity.

Loaded Words

Some words contain positive or negative connotations. Try to avoid them when you make an argument. Your readers may think you are trying to appeal to them by using these emotionally packed words. In fact, you want to persuade the reader by using logical arguments, not emotional rants.

Example:	The blue-flag freedom fighters won the war against the green-flag guerrillas.
Problem:	The terms *freedom fighters* (positive) and *guerrillas* (negative) may influence the readers' opinion about the two groups without any support for the bias.

Either/Or *Arguments*

When you argue a point, be careful not to limit the outcome choices to only two or three. In fact, there are often a multitude of choices. When you offer only two scenarios, you are essentially trying to frighten the reader into your beliefs.

Example: The instructor must either return the tests or dismiss the class.

Problem: This statement implies that only two choices are available to the instructor.

ACTIVITY 6 Faulty Logic

Read the following paragraph and underline all the uses of faulty logic. Write the kind of error each one is above the words.

Next week, our fine upstanding citizens will go to the polls to vote for or against a penny sales tax for construction of a new stadium. This law, if passed, will cause extreme hardship for local residents. Our taxes are high enough as it is, so why do our city's apathetic leaders think that we will run happily to the polls and vote "yes"? If we take a look at what happened to our sister city as a result of a similar bill, we will see that this new tax will have negative effects. Last year, that city raised its sales tax by one percent. Only three weeks later, the city was nearly destroyed by a riot in the streets. If we want to keep our fair city as it is, we must either vote "no" on the ballot question or live in fear of violence.

 For more practice with faulty logic, try Unit 5, Activity 6 on the *Great Writing 4* Web site: elt.heinle.com/greatwriting

---

✎ Writer's Note

Citing Sources to Avoid Plagiarism

When writing argumentative essays, it is often helpful to find facts, figures, or quotes to help support your ideas. With the ease of the Internet, however, we may forget to give credit to the person (or article or Web site) that the information came from. **Plagiarism**—whether done intentionally or unintentionally—is the act of taking others' words without properly giving credit to the source. Plagiarism is considered a very serious offense in academia and should be avoided at all costs.

After you have decided that the information you have found in a source is appropriate to support your ideas, you need to insert it in your essay correctly. There are two choices.

1. **Quoting** If the information is not too long, you can put it in quotation marks. It is a good idea to introduce the quote with a phrase, such as *According to (name of source), "(exact words used by that source)."* By using this strategy, you not only acknowledge the source but also show that the information is taken word for word. Be careful, however, not to use too many quotations in any particular paragraph. Remember, the reader is looking for *your* voice, not someone else's.

Example of quoting:

> According to http://www.webhealth.org, "Children need between three and six servings of vegetables daily to maintain a healthy diet."

2. **Paraphrasing**   Another method of avoiding plagiarism is to paraphrase your source's information. That is, you put the information in your own words. You still need to explain where the information came from even if you changed the words, but you do not need to use quotation marks.

Example of paraphrasing:

> According to http://www.webhealth.org, in order for a diet to be considered healthy, kids should eat a fair number of vegetables daily.

Your instructor can help you if you are unsure of when, where, or exactly how to cite information. In addition, librarians and other school support services often have extensive information on methods of avoiding plagiarism. The key to using outside sources correctly is to be diligent in citing the source you use and to ask questions if you are unsure of how to complete this task. For more information on citing sources, see the Brief Writer's Handbook with Activities, pages 157–159.

Building Better Vocabulary

ACTIVITY 7 Word Associations

Circle the word or phrase that is most closely related to the word or phrase on the left. If necessary, use a dictionary to check the meaning of words you do not know.

1. fundamental	important	not important
2. truancy	teachers	students
3. to implement	to put into effect	to stop using
4. pivotal	interesting	important
5. an amendment	to keep the same	to make a change
6. reluctant	to want to do to something	to not want to do something
7. outlawed	legal	illegal
8. antiquated	old	modern
9. an excerpt	a topic	a portion
10. to take into account	to consider	to recommend

Fill in each blank with the word on the left that most naturally completes the phrase on the right. If necessary, use a dictionary to check the meaning of words you do not know.

1. fire / screams   to come under _____

2. through / with   to be associated _____

3. dictionaries / community   a sense of _____

4. apartment / expression   individual _____

5. arms / telephones   to bear _____

6. in / off   She is better _____ taking a taxi.

7. do / make   to _____ some changes

8. fact / risk   to lower the _____

9. living / working   standard of _____

10. by / of   in fear _____

Original Student Writing: Argumentative Essay

Brainstorming

Brainstorming will help you get started with your argumentative essay. In this section, you will choose any method of brainstorming that works for you and develop supporting information.

ACTIVITY 9 Choosing a Topic

Follow the steps below to develop ideas for an argumentative essay.

1. First, choose a thesis statement from the statements that you wrote in Activity 5 on pages 120–121 or choose any other topic and thesis statement that you want to write about. Remember that the topic must have more than one point of view to qualify as an argument.

   Essay topic: _____

   Thesis statement: _____

   _____

2. Now brainstorm ideas about your topic. Write everything you can think of that supports your argument. You may want to begin by answering this question about your thesis statement: *Why do I believe this?*

3. Look at your brainstorming information again. Choose three or four reasons that support your thesis most effectively and circle them. You now know what your major supporting information will be.

4. Now that you have written your thesis statement and a few reasons to support it, it is time to give attention to opposing points of view. On the lines below, write one counterargument and a refutation for your argumentative essay.

   Counterargument: _____

   _____

   _____

   Refutation: _____

   _____

   _____

5. Remember to include a restatement of your thesis and your opinion about the issue in your conclusion.

ACTIVITY 10 Planning with an Outline

Complete the following outline as a guide to help you brainstorm a more detailed plan for your argumentative essay. Use your ideas from Activity 9. You may need to use either more or fewer points under each heading. Write complete sentences where possible.

Topic: _____

  I. Introduction (Paragraph 1)

   A. Hook: _____

   B. Connecting information: _____

   _____

C. Thesis statement: _____

_____

II. Body

   A. Paragraph 2 (first reason) topic sentence: _____

_____

SUPPORT

     1. _____

     2. _____

     3. _____

   B. Paragraph 3 (second reason) topic sentence: _____

_____

SUPPORT

     1. _____

     2. _____

     3. _____

   C. Paragraph 4 (third reason) topic sentence: _____

_____

SUPPORT

     1. _____

     2. _____

     3. _____

   D. Paragraph 5 (counterargument and refutation)

     1. Counterargument: _____

SUPPORT

_____

     2. Refutation: _____

_____

III. Conclusion (paragraph 6)

   A. Restated thesis:

_____

_____

   B. Opinion:

_____

_____

ACTIVITY 11 Peer Editing Your Outline

Exchange books with a partner and look at Activity 10. Read your partner's outline. Then use Peer Editing Sheet 7 on page 197 to help you comment on your partner's outline. Use your partner's feedback to revise your outline. Make sure you have enough information to develop your supporting sentences.

ACTIVITY 12 Writing an Argumentative Essay

Write an argumentative essay based on your revised outline from Activity 11. Use at least five of the vocabulary words or phrases presented in Activity 7 and Activity 8. Underline these words and phrases in your essay. Be sure to refer to the seven steps in the writing process in the Brief Writer's Handbook with Activities on pages 131–138.

ACTIVITY 13 Peer Editing Your Essay

Exchange papers from Activity 12 with a partner. Read your partner's writing. Then use Peer Editing Sheet 8 on page 199 to help you comment on your partner's writing. Be sure to offer positive suggestions and comments that will help your partner improve his or her writing. Consider your partner's comments as you revise your own writing.

Additional Topics for Writing

Here are more ideas for topics for an argumentative essay. Before you write, be sure to refer to the seven steps in the writing process in the Brief Writer's Handbook with Activities, pages 131–138.

TOPIC 1: The media often place heavy emphasis on the opinions and actions of celebrities, such as actors and sports stars. Should we pay attention to these opinions and actions? Are they important or not? Choose one side of this argument and write your essay in support of it.

TOPIC 2: At what age should a person be considered an adult? Make a decision about this issue and then argue your point of view. Do not forget to include a counterargument and refutation.

TOPIC 3: Consider the issue of school attendance policies. Do you think that students should be penalized for missing classes? Write an essay explaining your opinion.

TOPIC 4: Should a passing score on an English achievement test be the main requirement for international students to enter a university in an English-speaking country? What are the pros and cons of this issue? Choose one side and write your essay in support of it.

TOPIC 5: Is day care beneficial for children under the age of five? Should one parent stay home with children for the first few years of life? Develop a thesis statement about some aspect of the day-care-versus-home-care issue and support it in your argumentative essay.

How quickly can you write in English? There are many times when you must write quickly, such as on a test. It is important to feel comfortable during those times. Timed-writing practice can make you feel better about writing quickly in English.

First, read the essay guidelines below. Then take out a piece of paper. Read the writing prompt below the guidelines. As quickly as you can, write a basic outline for this writing prompt (including the thesis and your main points). You should spend <u>no more than</u> 5 minutes on your outline.

You will then have 40 minutes to write an argumentative essay about your topic. At the end of the 40 minutes, your teacher will collect your work and return it to you at a later date.

Argumentative Essay Guidelines

- Be sure to include a counterargument and a refutation.

- Remember to give your essay a title.

- Double-space your essay.

- Write as legibly as possible (if you are not using a computer).

- Include a short introduction (with a thesis statement), body paragraphs, and a conclusion.

- Try to give yourself a few minutes before the end of the activity to review your work. Check for spelling, verb tense, and subject-verb agreement mistakes.

What should happen to students who are caught cheating on an exam? Why?

Brief Writer's Handbook with Activities

Understanding the Writing Process: The Seven Steps

This section can be studied at any time during the course. You will want to refer to these seven steps many times as you write your essays.

The Assignment

Imagine that you have been given the following assignment: *Write an essay in which you discuss one aspect of vegetarianism.* What should you do first? What should you do second, third, and so on? There are many ways to write, but most good writers follow certain steps in the writing process. These steps are guidelines that are not always followed in order.

Look at this list of steps. Which ones do you regularly do? Which ones have you never done?

STEP 1: Choose a topic.

STEP 2: Brainstorm.

STEP 3: Outline.

STEP 4: Write the first draft.

STEP 5: Get feedback from a peer.

STEP 6: Revise the first draft.

STEP 7: Proofread the final draft.

Next, you will see how one student, Hamda, went through the steps to do the assignment. First, read the final essay that Hamda gave her teacher.

EXAMPLE ESSAY 22

Better Living as a Vegetarian

1   The hamburger has become a worldwide cultural icon. Eating meat, especially beef, is an integral part of many diverse cultures. Studies show, however, that the consumption of large quantities of meat is a major contributing factor toward a great many deaths, including the unnecessarily high number of deaths from heart-related problems. Although it has caught on slowly in western society, vegetarianism is a way of life that can help improve not only the quality of people's lives but also their longevity.

2   Surprising as it may sound, vegetarianism can have beneficial effects on the environment. Because demand for meat animals is so high, cattle are being raised in areas where rain forests once stood. As rain forest land is cleared in order to make room for cattle ranches, the environmental balance is upset; this imbalance could have serious consequences for humans. The article "Deforestation: The hidden cause of global warming" by Daniel Howden explains that much of the current global warming is due to depletion of the rain forests.

3 More important at an individual level is the question of how eating meat affects a person's health. Meat, unlike vegetables, can contain very large amounts of fat. Eating this fat has been connected—in some research cases—to certain kinds of cancer. In fact, *The St. Petersburg Times* reports, "There was a statistically significant risk for . . . gastric cancer associated with consumption of all meat, red meat and processed meat" (Rao, 2006). If people cut down on the amounts of meat they ate, they would automatically be lowering their risks of disease. Furthermore, eating animal fat can lead to obesity, and obesity can cause numerous health problems. For example, obesity can cause people to slow down and their heart to have to work harder. This results in high blood pressure. Meat is also high in cholesterol, and this only adds to health problems. With so much fat consumption worldwide, it is no wonder that heart disease is a leading killer.

4 If people followed vegetarian diets, they would not only be healthier but also live longer. Eating certain kinds of vegetables, such as broccoli, brussels sprouts, and cauliflower, has been shown to reduce the chance of contracting colon cancer later in life. Vegetables do not contain the "bad" fats that meat does. Vegetables do not contain cholesterol, either. Furthermore, native inhabitants of areas of the world where people eat more vegetables than meat, notably certain areas of the former Soviet Asian republics, routinely live to be over one hundred.

5 Some people argue that, human nature being what it is, it is unhealthy for humans to not eat meat. These same individuals say that humans are naturally carnivores and cannot help wanting to consume a juicy piece of red meat. However, anthropologists have shown that early humans ate meat only when other foods were not abundant. Man is inherently a herbivore, not a carnivore.

6 Numerous scientific studies have shown the benefits of vegetarianism for people in general. There is a common thread for those people who switch from eating meat to consuming only vegetable products. Although the change of diet is difficult at first, most never regret their decision to become a vegetarian. They feel better, and those around them comment that they look better than ever before. As more and more people are becoming aware of the risks associated with meat consumption, they too will make the change.

Steps in the Writing Process
Step 1: Choose a Topic

For this assignment, the topic was given: Write an essay on vegetarianism. As you consider the assignment topic, you have to think about what kind of essay you may want to write. Will you list different types of vegetarian diets? Will you talk about the history of vegetarianism? Will you argue that vegetarianism is or is not better than eating animal products?

Hamda chose to write an argumentative essay about vegetarianism to try to convince readers of its benefits. The instructor had explained that this essay was to be serious in nature and have facts to back up the claims made.

Step 2: Brainstorm

The next step for Hamda was to brainstorm.

In this step, you write every idea that pops into your head about your topic. Some of these ideas will be good, and some will be bad; write them all. The main purpose of brainstorming is to write as many ideas as you can think of. If one idea looks especially good, you might circle that idea or put a check next to it. If you write an idea and you know right away that you are not going to use it, you can cross it out.

Brainstorming methods include making lists, clustering similar ideas (see Unit 2), or diagramming your thoughts (see Unit 3).

Look at Hamda's brainstorming diagram on the topic of vegetarianism.

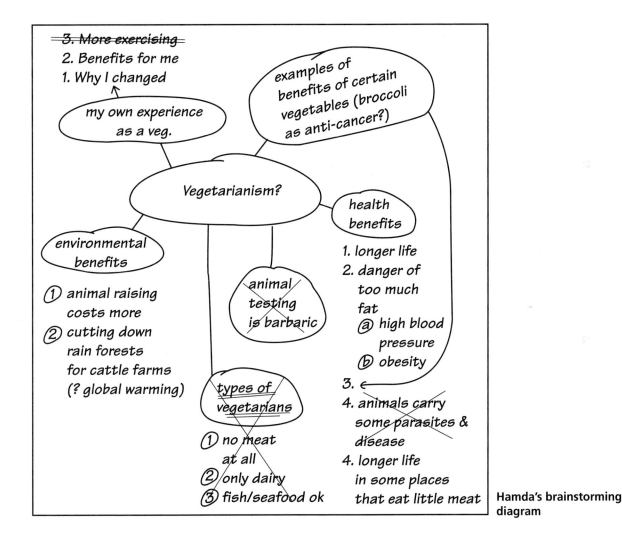

Hamda's brainstorming diagram

As you can see from the brainstorming diagram, Hamda considered many aspects of vegetarianism. Notice a few items in the diagram. As she organized her brainstorming, Hamda wrote "examples of benefits of certain vegetables" as a spoke on the wheel. Then she realized that this point would be a good number 3 in the list of benefits, so she drew an arrow to show that she should move it there. Since one of Hamda's brainstorming ideas (types of vegetarians), seemed to lack supporting details and was not related to her other notes, she crossed it out.

Getting the Information

How would you get the information for this brainstorming exercise?

- You might read a book or an article about vegetarianism.

- You could spend time in a library looking for articles on the subject.

- You could write a short questionnaire to give to classmates asking them about their personal knowledge of vegetarian practices.

- You could also interview an expert on the topic, such as a nutritionist.

✎ Writer's Note

Doing Research

To get a deeper understanding of your essay topic, you may choose to do some research. Remember, however, that any information you get from an outside source needs to be noted in your essay as an outside source. Writers do NOT use others' ideas in their writing without giving the proper credit.

Take another look at Hamda's essay. Can you find the places where she used outside sources to back up her ideas?

NOTE: See the Citations and Plagiarism section of the Brief Writer's Handbook with Activities on pages 157–159 for more information on citing outside sources and referencing.

Step 3: Outline

Next, create an outline for the essay. Here is Hamda's rough outline that she wrote from her brainstorming notes.

I. Introduction
   A. Define vegetarianism
   B. List different types
   C. Thesis statement

II. Environmental benefits (Find sources to support!)
   A. Rain forests
   B. Global warming

III. Health issues (Find sources to support!)
   A. Too much fat from meat → obesity → diseases → cancer
   B. High blood pressure and heart disease
   C. Cancer-fighting properties of broccoli and cauliflower, etc.

IV. Counterargument and refutation

    A. Counterargument: Man is carnivore.

    B. Refutation

V. Conclusion

    A. Restate thesis

    B. Opinion: Life will improve.

Supporting Details   After you have chosen the main points for your essay, you will need to develop some supporting details. You should include examples, reasons, explanations, definitions, or personal experiences. In some cases, such as this argumentative essay on vegetarianism, it is a good idea to include outside sources or expert opinions that back up your claims.

One common technique for generating supporting details is to ask specific questions about the topic, for example:

SUPPORT

What is it?

What happened?

How did this happen?

What is it like or not like? Why?

Step 4: Write the First Draft

Next, Hamda wrote her first draft. As she wrote each paragraph of the essay, she paid careful attention to the language she used. She chose a formal sentence structure including a variety of sentence types. In addition, her sentences varied in length, with the average sentence containing almost twenty words. (Sentences in conversation tend to be very short; sentences in academic writing tend to be longer.) Hamda also took great care in choosing appropriate vocabulary. In addition to specific terminology, such as *obesity*, *blood pressure*, and *consumption*, she avoided the conversational *you* in the essay, instead referring to *people* and *individuals*.

In this step, you use information from your brainstorming session and outline to write the essay. This first draft may contain many errors, such as misspellings, incomplete ideas, and comma errors. At this point, you should not worry about correcting the errors. The main thing is to put your ideas into sentences.

You may feel that you do not know what you think about the topic yet. In this case, it may be difficult for you to write, but it is important to just write, no matter what comes out. Sometimes writing helps you think, and as soon as you form a new thought, you can write it.

Better Living as a Vegetarian

Wow — too abrupt? You don't talk about hamburgers anymore??

~~Do you like hamburgers?~~ Eating meat, especially beef, is an interesting part of the *vocabulary?*

daily life around the world. In addition, this high ~~eating~~ of meat is a major contributing *word choice?*

factor ~~thing~~ that ~~makes~~ *causes* a great many deaths, including the unnecessarily high number of

deaths from heart-related problems. Vegetarianism has caught on slowly in some parts

of the world. ~~Vegetarianism~~ *, and it* is a way of life that can help improve not only the quality of

people's lives but also people's longevity. → *the quality but also the length of people's lives*

This is not a topic sentence Because demand for meat animals is ~~so high.~~ Cattle are being raised in areas where

the rainforest once stood. As rain forest land is cleared in massive amounts in order to

make room for the cattle ranches, the environmental balance is being upset. This could

For example, *transition?*

have serious consequences for us in both the near and long term. How much of the current

global warming is due to man's disturbing the rain forest?

You need a more specific topic relating to health.

Meat contains a high amount of fat. Eating this fat has been connected in research

cases with certain kinds of cancer. Furthermore, eating animal fat can lead to obesity, and

obesity can cause many different kinds of diseases, for example, obesity can cause people to

slow down and their heart to have to word harder. This results in high blood pressure.

Meat is high in cholesterol, and this only adds to the health problems. With the high

consumption of animal fat by so many people, it is no wonder that heart disease is a

leading killer.

Hamda's first draft

On the other hand, eating a vegetarian diet can improve a person's health. And

necessary?

vegetables taste so good. In fact, it can even save someone's life. Eating certain kinds

of vegetables, such as broccoli, brussel sprouts, and cauliflower, has been shown to

reduce the chance of having colon cancer later in life. *combine sentences?* Vegetables do not contain

the "bad" fats that meat does. Vegetables do not contain cholesterol, either. Native

inhabitants of areas of the world where mostly vegetables are consumed, notably

certain areas of the former Soviet republics, routinely live to be over one hundred.

good sentence Although numerous scientific studies have shown the benefits of vegetarianism for people

in general, I know firsthand how my life has improved since I decided to give up meat entirely.

In 2006, I saw a TV program that discussed problems connected to animals that are raised for

food. The program showed how millions of chickens are raised in dirty, crowded conditions

not related to your topic

until they are killed. The program also talked about how diseases can be spread from cow or

pig to humans due to unsanitary conditions. Shortly after I saw this show, I decided to try life

without eating meat. Although it was difficult at first, I have never regretted my decision to

become a vegetarian. I feel better and my friends tell me that I look better than ever before

Being a vegetarian has many benefits. Try it.

This is too short! How about making a prediction or suggestion for the reader. The previous paragraph told how the writer became a vegetarian, so doesn't it make sense for the conclusion to say something like "I'm sure your life will be better too if you become a vegetarian"?

I like this essay. You really need to work on the conclusion.

Making Changes   As you write the first draft, you may want to add information or take some out. In some cases, your first draft may not follow your outline exactly. That is OK. Writers do not always stick with their original plan or follow the steps in the writing process in order. Sometimes they go back and forth between steps. The writing process is much more like a cycle than a line.

Reread Hamda's first draft with her teacher's comments.

First Draft Tips   Here are some things to remember about the first draft copy:

- The first draft is not the final copy. Even native speakers who are good writers do not write an essay only one time. They rewrite as many times as necessary until the essay is the best that it can be.

- It is OK for you to make notes on your drafts; you can circle words, draw connecting lines, cross out words, or write new information. Make notes to yourself about what to change, what to add, or what to reconsider.

- If you cannot think of a word or an idea as you write, leave a blank space or circle. Then go back and fill in the space later. If you write a word that you know is not the right one, circle or underline it so you can fill in the right word later. Do not stop writing. When people read your draft, they can see these areas you are having trouble with and offer comments that may help.

- Do not be afraid to throw some sentences away if they do not sound right. Just as a good housekeeper throws away unnecessary things from the house, a good writer throws out unnecessary or wrong words or sentences.

The handwriting in the first draft is usually not neat. Sometimes it is so messy that only the writer can read it! Use a word-processing program, if possible, to make writing and revising easier.

Step 5: Get Feedback from a Peer

Hamda used Peer Editing Sheet 8 to get feedback on her essay draft. Peer editing is important in the writing process. You do not always see your own mistakes or places where information is missing because you are too close to the essay that you created. Ask someone to read your draft and give you feedback about your writing. Choose someone that you trust and feel comfortable with. While some people feel uneasy about peer editing, the result is almost always a better essay. Remember to be polite when you edit another student's paper.

Step 6: Revise the First Draft

This step consists of three parts:

1. React to the comments on the peer editing sheet.

2. Reread the essay and make changes.

3. Rewrite the essay one more time.

Step 7: Proofread the Final Draft

Most of the hard work is over now. In this step, the writer pretends to be a brand-new reader who has never seen the essay before. Proofread your essay for grammar, punctuation, and spelling errors and to see if the sentences flow smoothly.

Read Hamda's final paper again on pages 131–132.

Of course, the very last step is to turn the paper in to your teacher and hope that you get a good grade!

✏ Writer's Note

Proofreading

One good way to proofread your essay is to first set it aside for several hours or a day or two. The next time you read your essay, your head will be clearer and you will be more likely to see any problems. In fact, you will read the composition as another person would.

Editing Your Writing

While you must be comfortable writing quickly, you also need to be comfortable with improving your work. Writing an assignment is never a one-step process. For even the most gifted writers, it is often a multiple-step process. When you were completing your assignments in this book, you probably made some changes to your work to make it better. However, you may not have fixed all of the errors. The paper that you turned in to your teacher is called a **first draft**, which is sometimes referred to as a **rough draft**.

A first draft can often be improved. One way to improve an essay is to ask a classmate, friend, or teacher to read it and make suggestions. Your reader may discover that one of your paragraphs is missing a topic sentence, that you have made grammar mistakes, or that your essay needs better vocabulary choices. You may not always like or agree with the comments from a reader, but being open to changes will make you a better writer.

This section will help you become more familiar with how to identify and correct errors in your writing.

Step 1

Below is a student's first draft for a timed writing. The writing prompt for this assignment was "For most people, quitting a job is a very difficult decision. Why do people quit their jobs?" As you read the first draft, look for areas that need improvement and write your comments. For example, does the writer use the correct verb tenses? Is the punctuation correct? Is the vocabulary suitable for the intended audience? Does the essay have an appropriate hook?

There Are Many Reasons Why People Quit Their Jobs

Joann quit her high-paying job last week. She had had enough of her coworkers' abuse. Every day they would make fun of her and talk about her behind her back. Joann's work environment was too stressful, so she quit. Many employees quit their jobs. In fact, there are numerous reasons for this phenomenon.

First, the job does not fit the worker. Job seekers may accept a job without considering their skills. Is especially true when the economy is slowing and jobs are hard to find. The workers may try their best to change themselves depending on the work. However, at some point they realize that they are not cut out in this line of work and end up quitting. This lack of understanding or ability make people feel uncomfortable in their jobs. So they begin to look for other work.

Another reason people quit their jobs is the money. Why do people work in the first place? They work in order to make money. If employees are underpaid, he cannot earn enough to support himself or his family. The notion of working, earning a decent salary, and enjoy life is no longer possible. In this case, low-paid workers have no choice but to quit their jobs and search for a better-paying position.

Perhaps the biggest situation that leads people to quit their jobs is personality conflicts. It is really difficult for an employee to wake up every morning, knowing that they will be spending the next eight or nine hours in a dysfunctional environment. The problem can be with bosses or coworkers but the result is the same. Imagine working for a discriminate boss or colleagues which spread rumors. The stress levels increases until that employee cannot stand the idea of going to work. The employee quits his or her job in the hope of finding a more calm atmosphere somewhere else.

Work should not be a form of punishment. For those people who have problems with not feeling comfortable on the job, not getting paid enough, and not respected, it *does* feel like punishment. As a result, they quit and continue their search for a job that will give them a sense of pride, safety, and friends.

Step 2

Read the teacher comments on the first draft of "There Are Many Reasons Why People Quit Their Jobs." Are these the same things that you noticed?

The title should NOT be a complete sentence.

There Are Many Reasons Why People Quit Their Jobs

Consider changing your hook/introduction. The introduction here is already explaining one of the reasons for quitting a job. This information should be in the body of the essay. Suggestion: Use a "historical" hook describing how people were more connected to their jobs in the past than they are now.

Joann quit her high-paying job last week. She had had enough of her coworkers' abuse. Every

day they would make fun of her and talk about her behind her back. Joann's work environment

was too stressful, so she quit. Many employees quit their jobs. In fact, there are numerous reasons

for this phenomenon.

Try to use another transition phrase instead of first, second, etc.

add transition

(First,) the job does not fit the worker. ∧Job seekers may accept a job without considering their

word choice—be more specific   fragment

(skills.) Is especially true when the economy is slowing and jobs are hard to find. The workers may

word choice—better: "adapt to"

try their best to (change themselves depending on) the work. However, at some point they realize

prep

that they are not cut out (in) this line of work and end up quitting. This lack of understanding or

S-V agreement   fragment

ability (make) people feel uncomfortable in their (jobs. So) they begin to look for other work.

word choice—be more specific

Another reason people quit their jobs is the (money.) Why do people work in the first place?

They work in order to make money. If (employees) are underpaid, (he) cannot earn enough to

pronoun agreement

// not parallel—use "-ing"

support (himself) or (his family.) The notion of working, earning a decent salary, and (enjoy) life is

word choice   Do you mean "underpaid"?

no longer (possible.) In this case, (low-paid) workers have no choice but to quit their jobs and

search for a better-paying position.

word choice—too vague

Perhaps the (biggest) situation that leads people to quit their jobs is personality conflicts. It is

word choice—avoid using "really"   *pronoun agreement*

(really) difficult for an employee to wake up every morning, knowing that (they) will be spending

add another descriptive word here   *word choice—too vague*

the next eight or nine hours in a dysfunctional ∧ environment. The (problem) can be with bosses

punc. (add comma)   *word choice*

or coworkers but the result is the same. Imagine working for a (discriminate) boss or colleagues

word form   *S-V agreement*   *write it out—better: "can no longer"*

(which) spread rumors. The stress levels (increases) until that employee (can't) stand the idea of

add transition   *word choice—better: "serene"*

going to work. ∧ The employee quits his or her job in the hope of finding a more (calm) atmosphere

somewhere else.

thought of as   *word choice*

Work should not be ∧ a form of punishment. For those people who (have problems) with not

// not parallel—use "-ing"

feeling comfortable on the job, not getting paid enough, and (not respected,) it *does* feel like

punishment. As a result, they quit and continue their search for a job that will give them a

word choice—better: "camaraderie"

sense of pride, safety, and (friends.)

Step 3

Now read the second draft of this essay. How is it the same as the first draft? How is it different? Did the writer fix all the sentence mistakes?

Two Weeks' Notice

A generation ago, it was common for workers to stay at their place of employment for years and years. When it was time for these employees to retire, companies would offer a generous pension package and, sometimes, a token of appreciation, such as a watch, keychain, or other trinket. Oh, how times have changed. Nowadays, people—especially younger workers—jump from job to job like bees fly from flower to flower to pollinate. Some observers might say that today's workforce is not as serious as yesterday's. This is too simple an explanation, however. In today's society, fueled by globalization, recession, and other challenges, people quit their jobs for a number of valid reasons.

One reason for quitting a job is that the job does not fit the worker. In other words, job seekers may accept a job without considering their aptitude for it. This is especially true when the economy is slowing and jobs are hard to find. The workers may try their best to adapt themselves to the work. However, at some point they realize that they are not cut out for this line of work and end up quitting. This lack of understanding or ability makes people feel uncomfortable in their jobs, so they begin to look for other work.

Another reason people quit their jobs is the salary. Why do people work in the first place? They work in order to make money. If employees are underpaid, they cannot earn enough to support themselves or their families. The notion of working, earning a decent salary, and enjoying life is no longer viable. In this case, underpaid workers have no choice but to quit their jobs and search for a better-paying position.

Perhaps the most discouraging situation that leads people to quit their jobs is personality conflicts. It is extremely difficult for an employee to wake up every morning knowing that he or she will be spending the next eight or nine hours in a dysfunctional and often destructive environment. The discord can be with bosses or coworkers, but the result is the same. Imagine working for a bigoted boss or colleagues who spread rumors. The stress levels increase until that employee can no longer stand the idea of going to work. In the end, the employee quits his or her job with the hope of finding a more serene atmosphere somewhere else.

Work should not be thought of as a form of punishment. For those people who struggle with not feeling comfortable on the job, not getting paid enough, and not being respected, it *does* feel like punishment. As a result, they quit and continue their search for a job that will give them a sense of pride, safety, and camaraderie.

Sentence Types

English sentence structure includes three basic types of sentences: **simple**, **compound**, and **complex**. These labels indicate how the information in a sentence is organized, not how difficult the content is.

Simple Sentences

1. Simple sentences usually contain one subject and one verb.

     s   v

    Kids love television.

   v   s   v

   Does this sound like a normal routine?

2. Sometimes simple sentences can contain more than one subject or verb.

         s   v

   Brazil and the United States are large countries.

   s   v   v

   Brazil lies in South America and has a large population.

   s   v   v

   We traveled throughout Brazil and ended our trip in Argentina.

Compound Sentences

Compound sentences are usually made up of two simple sentences (independent clauses). Compound sentences need a coordinating conjunction (connector) to combine the two sentences. The coordinating conjunctions include:

   for   and   nor   but   or   yet   so

Many writers remember these conjunctions with the acronym *FANBOYS*. Each letter represents one conjunction: *F = for, A = and, N = nor, B = but, O = or, Y = yet*, and *S = so*.

Remember that a comma is always used before a coordinating conjunction that separates the two independent clauses.

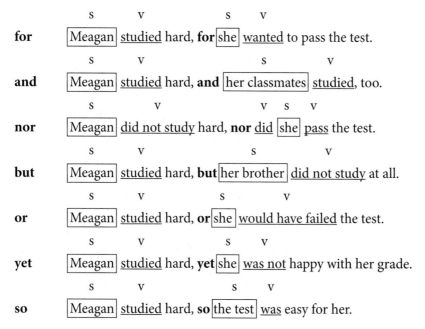

for   Meagan studied hard, **for** she wanted to pass the test.

and   Meagan studied hard, **and** her classmates studied, too.

nor   Meagan did not study hard, **nor** did she pass the test.

but   Meagan studied hard, **but** her brother did not study at all.

or   Meagan studied hard, **or** she would have failed the test.

yet   Meagan studied hard, **yet** she was not happy with her grade.

so   Meagan studied hard, **so** the test was easy for her.

Activity 1

Study the following examples of compound sentences. Draw a box *around each subject,* underline *each verb, and* circle *each coordinating conjunction.*

1. Brazil was colonized by Europeans, and its culture has been greatly influenced by this fact.

2. This was my first visit to the international section of the airport, and nothing was familiar.

3. Many people today are overweight, and being overweight has been connected to some kinds of cancer.

4. Barriers fell, markets opened, and people rejoiced in the streets because they anticipated a new life full of opportunities and freedom to make their own choices.

5. Should public school students make their own individual decisions about clothing, or should all students wear uniforms?

6. This question has been asked many times, but people are not in agreement about the ultimate punishment.

Complex Sentences

Like compound sentences, complex sentences are made up of two parts. Complex sentences, however, contain one independent clause and, at least, one dependent clause. In most complex sentences, the dependent clause is an adverb clause.

Complex Sentences (with Adverb Clauses)

Adverb clauses begin with subordinating conjunctions, which include the following:

while   although   after   because   if   before

Study the examples below. The adverb clauses are underlined, and the subordinating conjunctions are boldfaced.

The hurricane struck **while** we were at the mall.

After the president gave his speech, he answered most of the reporter's questions.

NOTE: A more complete list of subordinating conjunctions can be found in the Connectors section of the Brief Writer's Handbook with Activities, pages 156–157.

Unlike coordinating conjunctions, which join two independent clauses but are not part of either clause, subordinating conjunctions are actually part of the dependent clause.

Joe played tennis **after** Vicky watched TV.

INDEPENDENT CLAUSE   DEPENDENT CLAUSE

The subordinating conjunction *after* does not connect the clauses *Joe played tennis* and *Vicky watched TV; after* is grammatically part of *Vicky watched TV.*

Remember that dependent clauses must be attached to an independent clause. They cannot stand alone as a sentence. If they are not attached to another sentence, they are called fragments, or incomplete sentences. Fragments are incomplete ideas, and they cause confusion for the reader. In a complex sentence, both clauses are needed to make a complete idea so the reader can understand what you mean. Look at these examples:

Fragment:	After Vicky watched TV.
Complete Sentence:	Joe played tennis after Vicky watched TV.
	or
Complete Sentence:	After Vicky watched TV, she went to bed.

Activity 2

Study the following examples of complex sentences from the essays in this book. Draw a box *around each subject,* underline *each verb, and* circle *each subordinating conjunction.*

1. While the Northeast is experiencing snowstorms, cities like Miami, Florida, can have temperatures over 80 degrees Fahrenheit.

2. Although Brazil and the United States are unique countries, there are remarkable similarities in their size, ethnic diversity, and personal values.

3. Before the educational reforms occurred in Taiwan, non-academic achievements were not important for college entry.

4. If a sentence is grammatically incorrect, one of these programs highlights the incorrect parts of the sentence and corrects them.

5. Because almost every area has a community college, students who opt to go to a community college first can continue to be near their families for two more years.

Additional Grammar Activities

The three example essays in this section feature different grammatical errors. Each paragraph highlights one kind of error. In each case, read the entire essay before you complete the activities.

Before you complete Activities 1–5, read the whole essay first. Then go back and complete each activity.

Activity 1 Verb Forms

Read the paragraph and decide whether the 5 underlined verbs are correct. If not, draw a line through the verb and write the correct form above the verb.

EXAMPLE ESSAY 23

A Simple Recipe

1   "When in Rome, do as the Romans do" may <u>sound</u> ridiculous, but this proverb <u>offer</u> an important suggestion. If you travel to other countries, especially to a country that is very different from your own, you should <u>keeping</u> this saying in mind. For example, Japan has unique customs that <u>is</u> not found in any other country. If you <u>traveled</u> to Japan, you should find out about Japanese customs, taboos, and people beforehand.

Activity 2 Verb Forms

Read this paragraph carefully. Then write the correct form of the verbs in parentheses.

2   One custom is that you should (take) _____ off your shoes before (enter) _____ someone's house. In Japan, the floor must always be kept clean because usually people (sit) _____, eat a meal, or even (sleep) _____ on the floor. Another custom is giving gifts. The Japanese often (give) _____ a small gift to people who have (do) _____ favors for them. Usually this token of gratitude (give) _____ in July and December to keep harmonious relations with the receiver. When you (give) _____ someone such a gift, you should make some form of apology about it. For example, many Japanese will say, "This is just a small gift that I have for you." In addition, it is not polite to open a gift immediately. The receiver usually (wait) _____ until the giver has left so the giver will not be embarrassed if the gift (turn) _____ out to be defective or displeasing.

Activity 3 Connectors

Read the paragraph carefully. Then fill in the blanks with one of these connectors:

because   in addition   even if   for example   first   but

3   _____, it is important to know about Japanese taboos. All cultures have certain actions that are considered socially unacceptable. _____ something is acceptable in one culture, it can easily be taboo in another culture. _____, chopsticks are used in many cultures, _____ there are two taboos about chopsticks etiquette in Japan. _____, you should never stand the chopsticks upright in your bowl of rice. _____ standing chopsticks upright is done at a funeral ceremony, this action is associated with death. Second, you must never pass food from one pair of chopsticks to another. Again, this is related to burial rites in Japan.

Activity 4 Articles

There are 14 blanks in this paragraph. Read the paragraph and write the articles a, an, *or* the *to complete the sentences. Some blanks do not require articles.*

4   Third, it is important to know that Japanese people have _____ different cultural values. One of _____ important differences in _____ cultural values is _____ Japanese desire to maintain _____ harmony at all costs. People try to avoid causing any kind of dispute. If there is _____ problem, both sides are expected to compromise in order to avoid an argument. People are expected to restrain their emotions and put _____ goal of compromise above their individual wishes. Related to this is _____ concept of patience. Japanese put _____ great deal of _____ value on _____ patience. Patience also contributes to maintaining _____ good relations with _____ everyone and avoiding _____ disputes.

Activity 5 Prepositions

Read this paragraph and write the correct preposition in each blank. Choose from these prepositions: into, in, to, about, with, of, *and* around. *You may use them more than once.*

5   _____ conclusion, if you want to get along well _____ the Japanese and avoid uncomfortable situations when you go _____ Japan, it is important to take _____ account the features _____ Japanese culture that have been discussed here. Although it may be hard to understand Japanese customs because they are different, knowing _____ them can help you adjust to life in Japan. If you face an unfamiliar or difficult situation when you are _____ Japan, you should do what the people _____ you do. In other words, "When _____ Japan, do as the Japanese do."

Before you complete Activities 6–12, read the whole essay first. Then go back and complete each activity.

Activity 6 Verb Forms
Read this paragraph carefully. Then write the correct form of the verbs in parentheses.

Dangers of Corporal Punishment

1   What should parents do when their five-year-old child says a bad word even though the child knows it is wrong? What should a teacher (do) _____ when a student in the second grade (call) _____ the teacher a name? When my parents (be) _____ children forty or fifty years ago, the answer to these questions was quite clear. The adult would spank the child immediately. Corporal punishment (be) _____ quite common then. When I was a child, I (be) _____ in a class in which the teacher got angry at a boy who kept (talk) _____ after she told him to be quiet. The teacher then (shout) _____ at the boy and, in front of all of us, (slap) _____ his face. My classmates and I were shocked. Even after twenty years, I still remember that incident quite clearly. If the teacher's purpose (be) _____ to (teach) _____ us to (be) _____ quiet, she did not (succeed) _____. However, if her purpose was to create an oppressive mood in the class, she succeeded. Because corporal punishment (be) _____ an ineffective and cruel method of discipline, it should never be (use) _____ under any circumstances.

Activity 7 Prepositions
Read this paragraph carefully. Write the correct preposition in each blank. Use these prepositions: in, of, *and* for.

2   Supporters _____ corporal punishment claim that physical discipline is necessary _____ developing a child's sense _____ personal responsibility. Justice Lewis Powell, a former U.S. Supreme Court justice, has even said that paddling children who misbehave has been an acceptable method _____ promoting good behavior and responsibility _____ school children for a long time. Some people worry that stopping corporal punishment in schools could result _____ a decline _____ school achievement. However, just because a student stops misbehaving does not mean that he or she suddenly has a better sense _____ personal responsibility or correct behavior.

Activity 8 Articles

Read the paragraph and write the articles a, an, *or the* to *complete the sentences. Some blanks do not require articles.*

3   Corporal punishment is _____ ineffective way to punish _____ child because it may stop a behavior for a while, but it will not necessarily have _____ long-term effect. Thus, if an adult inflicts _____ mild form of _____ corporal punishment that hurts the child very little or not at all, it will not get rid of the bad behavior. Moreover, because corporal punishment works only temporarily, it will have to be repeated whenever the child misbehaves. It may then become _____ standard response to any misbehavior. This can lead to _____ frequent and more severe spanking, which may result in _____ abuse.

Activity 9 Comma Splices

Read this paragraph carefully and find the 2 comma splices. Correct them in one of two ways: (1) change the comma to a period and make two sentences or (2) add a connector after the comma.

4   A negative effect of corporal punishment in school is that it makes some students feel aggressive toward parents, teachers, and fellow students. In my opinion, children regard corporal punishment as a form of teacher aggression that makes them feel helpless. Therefore, students may get frustrated if corporal punishment is used frequently. Furthermore, it increases disruptive behavior that can become more aggressive, this leads to school violence and bullying of fellow students. Supporters of corporal punishment believe that it is necessary to maintain a good learning environment, it is unfortunate that the opposite result often happens. The learning environment actually becomes less effective when there is aggressive behavior.

Activity 10 Verb Forms

Read the paragraph and decide whether the underlined verbs are correct. If not, draw a line through the verb and write the correct form above it.

5   Last, corporal punishment may <u>result</u> in antisocial behavior later in life because it teaches children that adults <u>condone</u> violence as a solution to problems. Children who are <u>spank</u> learn that it is acceptable for a stronger person <u>using</u> violence against a weaker person. The concept of "might makes right" is <u>forced</u> upon them at a very early age. Furthermore, this concept teaches a lesson not only to those who are spanked but also to those who <u>witness</u> it. Studies of prisoners and delinquents <u>shows</u> that nearly 100 percent of the violent inmates at San Quentin and 64 percent of juvenile delinquents <u>was</u> victims of seriously abusive punishment during childhood. If serious punishment <u>causes</u> antisocial behavior, perhaps even milder punishment also <u>contribute</u> to violence. Research at the University of New Hampshire <u>will find</u> that children who were spanked between the ages of three and five <u>showed</u> higher levels of antisocial behavior when they <u>were observed</u> just two and four years later. This behavior included higher levels of beating family members, hitting fellow students, and defying parents. It is ironic that the behaviors for which teachers <u>punishing</u> students often get worse as a result of the spanking.

Activity 11 Editing for Errors

There are 7 errors in this paragraph. They are in word forms (2), articles (1), sentence fragments (1), verb tense (1), and subject-verb agreement (2). Mark these errors and write corrections.

6   For punishment to be effective, it must produce a great behavioral change, result in behavior that is permanent, and produce minimal side effects. However, none of these changes is a result of corporal punishment. Therefore, we should consider alternatives to corporal punishment. Because discipline is necessary to educate children. One of the alternatives are to emphasize students' positive behaviors. Some research shows that reward, praise, and self-esteem is the most powerful motivators for the learning. Other alternatives are to hold conferences with students to help them plan acceptable behave or to use school staff, such as psychologists and counselors. It is important to build better interpersonal relations between teachers and students. In addition to these alternatives, instruction that reaches all students, such as detention, in-school suspension, and Saturday school, is available to discipline and punishment unruly students, too. Alternatives to corporal punishment taught children to be self-disciplined rather than to be cooperative only because of fear.

Activity 12 Editing for Errors

There are 7 errors in this paragraph. They are in word forms (1), articles (3), sentence fragments (1), comma splices (1), and subject-verb agreement (1). Mark these errors and write the corrections.

7   In the conclusion, teachers should not use corporal punishment because it is ineffective in disciplining students and may have long-term negative effects on students. Moreover, teachers should not forget that love and understanding must be part of any kind of discipline. Discipline and love is not opposites, punishment must involve letting the children know that what they do is wrong and why punishment is necessary. Teachers should not just beat student with the hopeful that he will understand. It is important to maintain discipline without inflicting physical pain on students. Therefore, teachers should use effective and more humane alternatives. In order to bring about permanent behavioral changes.

Before you complete Activities 13–18, read the whole essay first. Then go back and complete each activity.

Activity 13 Articles

Read the paragraph and write the articles a, an, *or the* to *complete the sentences. Some blanks do not require articles.*

Washington and Lincoln

1 Perhaps no other names from _____ American history are better known than the names of George Washington and Abraham Lincoln. Both of these presidents made valuable contributions to _____ United States during their presidency. In fact, one could argue that _____ America would not be _____ same country that it is today if either of these two leaders had not been involved in _____ American politics. However, it is interesting to note that although both leaders made _____ significant contributions to _____ country, they lived in _____ quite different times and served in _____ very different ways.

Activity 14 Verb Forms

Read this paragraph carefully. Then write the correct form of the verbs in parentheses.

2 Everyone (know) _____ that George Washington was the first president of the United States. What most people do not (appreciate) _____ (be) _____ that Washington (be) _____ a clever military leader. He served the country in the early days of the Revolution by (help) _____ to change the colonial volunteers from ragged farmers into effective soldiers. Without Washington's bravery and military strategy, it is doubtful that the colonies could have (beat) _____ the British. Thus, without Washington, the colonies might never even have (become) _____ the United States of America.

Activity 15 Prepositions

Read this paragraph and write the correct preposition in each blank. Choose from these prepositions: from, in, to, with, for, between, *and* of. *You may use them more than once.*

3   Abraham Lincoln was the sixteenth president _____ the United States. He was elected president _____ 1860 during a controversial and heated period of American history. As more states applied _____ membership in the growing country, the issue _____ slavery kept surfacing. There was an unstable balance _____ slave states and free states. Each time another state was added _____ the Union, the balance of power shifted. Lincoln was _____ a free state, and many _____ the slave state leaders viewed Lincoln as an enemy of their cause _____ expand slavery. _____ the end, no compromise could be reached, and the slave states seceded _____ the United States in order to form their own independent country. Hostilities grew, and _____ 1861 the Civil War, or the War _____ the States as it is sometimes called, broke out. During the next four years, the Civil War ravaged the country. By the end of the war in 1865, the American countryside was _____ shambles, but the Union was once again intact. Through his military and political decisions, Lincoln is credited _____ saving the country _____ self-destruction.

Activity 16 Editing for Errors

There are 8 errors in this paragraph. They are in word forms (1), articles (2), modals (1), verb tense (2), and subject-verb agreement (2). Mark these errors and write corrections.

4   Washington and Lincoln was similarly in several ways. Both men are U.S. presidents. Both men served the United States during extremely difficult times. For Washington, the question is whether the United States would be able to maintain its independence from Britain. The United States was certainly very fragile nation at that time. For Lincoln, the question were really not so different. Would the United States to be able to survive during what was one of darkest periods of American history?

Activity 17 Sentence Fragments

After you read this paragraph, find the 3 sentence fragments. Correct the fragments by (1) changing the punctuation and creating one complete sentence or (2) adding new words to make the fragment a complete sentence.

5   There were also several differences between Washington and Lincoln. Washington came from a wealthy aristocratic background. He had several years of schooling. Lincoln came from a poor background, and he had very little schooling. Another difference between the two involved their military roles. Washington was a general. He was a military leader. Became president. Lincoln never served in the military. He was a lawyer who early on became a politician. When he became president, he took on the role of commander in chief, as all U.S. presidents do. Despite his lack of military background or training. Lincoln made several strategic decisions that enabled the U.S. military leaders to win the Civil War. Finally, Washington served for two terms and therefore had eight years to accomplish his policies. Lincoln, on the other hand, was assassinated. While in office and was not able to finish some of the things that he wanted for the country.

Activity 18 Editing for Errors

There are 7 errors in this paragraph. They are in articles (2), verb tense (1), inappropriate words (1), word forms (1), number (singular and plural) (1), and subject-verb agreement (1). Mark these errors and make corrections.

6   The names George Washington and Abraham Lincoln is known even to people who have never been to the United States. Both of these patriots gave large part of their lives to help America make what it is today though they served the country in very different ways in complete different time in the American history. Although they were gone, their legacies and contributions continue to have an impact on our lives.

Connectors

Using connectors will help your ideas flow. Remember that when connectors occur at the beginning of a sentence, they are often followed by a comma.

Purpose	Coordinating Conjunctions (connect independent clauses)	Subordinating Conjunctions (begin dependent clauses)	Transitions (usually precede independent clauses)
Examples			For example, To illustrate, Specifically, In particular,
Information	and		In addition, Moreover, Furthermore,
Comparison			Similarly, Likewise, In the same way,
Contrast	but	while although	In contrast, However, On the other hand, Conversely, Instead,
Refutation			On the contrary,
Concession	yet	although though even though it may appear that	Nevertheless, Even so, Admittedly, Despite this,
Emphasis			In fact, Actually,
Clarification			In other words, In simpler words, More simply,
Reason/Cause	for	because since	
Result	so	so so that	As a result, As a consequence, Consequently, Therefore, Thus,

Purpose	Coordinating Conjunctions (connect independent clauses)	Subordinating Conjunctions (begin dependent clauses)	Transitions (usually precede independent clauses)
Time Relationships		after as soon as before when while until whenever as	Afterward, First, Second, Next, Then Finally, Subsequently, Meanwhile, In the meantime,
Condition		if even if unless provided that when	
Purpose		so that in order that	
Choice	or		
Conclusion			In conclusion, To summarize, As we have seen, In brief, In closing, To sum up, Finally,

Citations and Plagiarism

Imagine this situation: You have invited some friends over for dinner. Because you did not have time to make a dessert, you stop at a local bakery and pick up a cake. After dinner, your friends compliment you on the delicious cake you made. How do you respond? Most people would give credit to the person who made the cake: "I'm glad you liked it, but I didn't make it. I bought it at Sunshine Bakery." By clarifying that the cake was not yours, you are rightfully giving the credit to Sunshine Bakery. The same concept holds true in writing.

When you write an essay, you should use your own words for the most part. Sometimes, however, writers want to use ideas that they have read in another piece of writing. For example, writers may want to use a quotation from a famous politician if they are writing an essay about a recent election. In this case, the writer must indicate that the idea or the words came from someone else and give credit to that writer. The action of indicating that a writer's words are not original but rather from another source is called **citing**. In academic writing, it is <u>imperative</u> for a writer to cite all information that is not original.

If writers do not give credit for borrowed ideas or borrowed words, they make a serious error. In fact, it is academic theft, and such stealing of ideas or words cannot be tolerated at all. It is not acceptable to use even a few words from another source without citing the source—the amount of information that you borrow is irrelevant. If you steal one sentence or one paragraph, it is still stealing. Stealing someone else's ideas or words and using them in a piece of writing as if they were the writer's original ideas is called **plagiarism**. In an academic setting, plagiarism is considered a very serious offense. In most schools, there are serious academic consequences for plagiarizing any work. For example, some schools require the paper to receive a score of 0 (zero). Other schools will expel the student permanently. In some instances, schools will take both of the above steps.

Does this mean then that writers cannot use other people's words or ideas? No, not at all. In fact, good writing can be strengthened further by using facts from outside sources or quotes from officials to support key points or ideas, so writers should borrow appropriate information. The key to avoiding plagiarism is to cite the source of the information.

Many students have a difficult time knowing when to use a citation, especially if they believe the information is general knowledge. For example, Hessa, a student from the United Arab Emirates (UAE), is writing an essay about her country. She knows that the UAE is made up of seven emirates. Does she need to cite this information? If Hessa is writing this essay in an English-speaking country where people may not know that there are seven emirates, she needs to cite the information. If, however, the information is common knowledge in Hessa's academic community, she would not have to cite the information. In the end, it is better to cite the information than to risk being accused of plagiarism. Before turning in any piece of writing, it is helpful to mark any information that is not your original writing. For any information that you mark, you need to give credit to the person, organization, or Web site that originally wrote it by citing the sources.

Citing: Using a Direct Quotation or Paraphrasing

When you use material from another source, you have two choices: using a **direct quotation** or **paraphrasing**. If a writer uses the exact words (a direct quotation) from a source, the borrowed words must be placed in quotation marks. If a writer borrows an idea from a source but uses his or her original words to express this idea, the writer has used a method called paraphrasing. Paraphrasing does not require quotation marks because the writer is not using the exact words from the original source. However, whether a writer is using an exact quotation or a paraphrased version, the information is not original and must be cited.

Example of a Direct Quotation

Notice that this paragraph from *Vocabulary Myths* (Folse, 2004) contains a direct quote. When you use a direct quote, you must state the name of the author, the date of the publication, and the page number of the direct quotation.

> One of the first observations that second language learners make in their new language is that they need vocabulary knowledge to function well in that language. How frustrating it is when you want to say something and are stymied because you do not know the word for a simple noun even! In spite of the obvious importance of vocabulary, most courses and curricula tend to be based on grammar or a combination of grammar and communication strategies rather than vocabulary. As a result, even after taking many courses, learners still lack sufficient vocabulary knowledge. Vocabulary knowledge is critical to any communication. Wilkins (1972) summarizes the situation best with "While without grammar very little can be conveyed, without vocabulary *nothing* can be conveyed" (p. 111).

Example of a Longer Quotation

Notice that this paragraph from *Vocabulary Myths* (Folse, 2004) contains a longer direct quote. In this case, the direct quotation is set off differently than original writing.

> As more and more empirical research in second language study is made available and results provide important insight into our questions about vocabulary learning and teaching, the education pendulum is swinging back toward some more "traditional" methods, including those which rely

on explicit instruction from the teacher. This in turn begs the question of what kinds of classroom activities, especially vocabulary activities, are effective for L2 learners. Carter and McCarthy (1988) conclude that

> although it suffered neglect for a long time, vocabulary pedagogy has benefited in the last fifteen years or so from theoretical advances in the linguistic lexicon, from psycholinguistic investigations into the mental lexicon, from the communicative trend in teaching, which has brought the learner into focus, and from developments in computers. What is perhaps missing in all this is more knowledge about what happens in classrooms when vocabulary crops up (p. 51).

Example of a Paraphrase

Notice that this paragraph from *Vocabulary Myths* (Folse, 2004) contains a paraphrase, or summary, of a concept from a work written by Eskey in 1988. Instead of using any phrases or sentences from Eskey's work, Folse uses a sentence in the paragraph that summarizes Eskey's work and connects that idea to the current paragraph and audience. When you paraphrase material, you must state the name of the author and the date of the publication.

> While lack of vocabulary knowledge is a problem across all skill areas, it is especially apparent in ESL reading. Eskey (1988) found that not being able to recognize the meaning of English words automatically causes students who are good readers in their native language to do excessive guesswork in the second language and that this guessing slows down the process of reading.

Bibliography

In addition to providing information on sources in places where they are used within your writing, you should also list all the works, or sources, of the words and ideas you used in the final **bibliography**, or list of works cited, at the end of your paper.

Citation methods vary according to academic professions and fields, so you should ask your instructor about the citation system that is required in your coursework.

Study the following example of a bibliography that lists the four works used in the preceding examples. The first, third, and fourth entries are books. The second entry is a chapter in an edited volume.

Bibliography

Carter, R., and M. McCarthy. 1988. *Vocabulary and language teaching.* New York: Longman.

Eskey, D. 1988. Holding in the bottom: An interactive approach to the language problems of second language readers. In *Interactive approaches to second language reading,* edited by P. Carrell, J. Deveine, J., and D. Eskey. Cambridge: Cambridge University Press.

Folse, K. 2004. *Vocabulary myths: Applying second language research to classroom teaching.* Ann Arbor: University of Michigan Press.

Wilkins, D. 1972. *Linguistics in language teaching.* London: Edward Arnold.

Appendices

Appendix 1

 Building Better Sentences

Being a good writer involves many skills, such as being able to use correct grammar, vary vocabulary usage, and state ideas concisely. Some student writers like to keep their sentences simple because they feel that if they create longer and more complicated sentences, they are more likely to make mistakes. However, writing short, choppy sentences one after the other is not considered appropriate in academic writing. Study these examples:

The time was yesterday.

It was afternoon.

There was a storm.

The storm was strong.

The movement of the storm was quick.

The storm moved towards the coast.

The coast was in North Carolina.

Notice that every sentence has an important piece of information. A good writer would not write all these sentences separately. Instead, the most important information from each sentence can be used to create one longer, coherent sentence.

Read the sentences again below and notice that the important information has been circled.

The time was (yesterday.)

It was (afternoon.)

There was a (storm.)

The storm was (strong.)

The (movement) of the storm was (quick.)

The storm moved towards the (coast.)

The coast was in (North Carolina.)

Here are some strategies for taking the circled information and creating a new sentence.

1. Create time phrases to introduce or end a sentence: *yesterday + afternoon*
2. Find the key noun: *storm*
3. Find key adjectives: *strong*
4. Create noun phrases: *a strong + storm*
5. Change word forms: *movement = move; quick = quickly*

    moved + quickly

6. Create prepositional phrases: *towards the coast*

    towards the coast (*of North Carolina*)

    or

    towards the North Carolina coast

Now read this improved, longer sentence:

    Yesterday afternoon, a strong storm moved quickly towards the North Carolina coast.

Here are some more strategies for building better sentences:

7. Use coordinating conjunctions (*and, but, or, nor, yet, for, so*) to connect two sets of ideas.

8. Use subordinating conjunctions, such as *after, while, since,* and *because,* to connect related ideas.

9. Use clauses with relative pronouns, such as *who, which, that,* and *whose,* to describe or define a noun or noun phrase.

10. Use pronouns to refer to previously mentioned information.

11. Use possessive adjectives and pronouns, such as *my, her, his, ours,* and *theirs.*

Study the following example.

(Susan) (went) somewhere. That place was (the mall.) Susan wanted to (buy new shoes.) The shoes were for (Susan's mother.)

Now read the improved, longer sentence:

Susan went to the mall because she wanted to buy new shoes for her mother.

Practices

This section contains practices for the example essays in Units 1–5. Follow these steps for each practice:

1. Read the sentences. Circle the most important information in each sentence.

2. Write an original sentence from the information you circled. Use the strategies listed above.

3. Go back to the original paragraph in the essay to check your sentence. Find the sentence in the paragraph. Compare your sentence with the original sentence. Remember that there is more than one way to combine sentences.

Note that the first exercise in Practice 1 has been done for you.

Practice 1 Unit 1, "Cinderella and Her Odious Household Chores," page 3

A. (Paragraph 3)

1. There is (another chore.)

2. The chore is in the (household.)

3. (Many people dislike) this chore.

4. The chore is (washing dishes.)

   Another household chore that many people dislike is washing dishes.

B. (Paragraph 4)

1. The bathroom is full of germs.

2. Because of this, a wiping is not enough.

3. The wiping is quick.

4. The wiping is of the surfaces.

_____

_____

C. (Paragraph 4)

    1. The task is so unpleasant.

    2. The task is cleaning the bathroom.

    3. Some people wear gloves when they attempt it.

    4. The gloves are made of rubber.

_____

_____

D. (Paragraph 5)

    1. Maintaining a house means doing something.

    2. The "something" is chores.

    3. There is a wide variety of chores.

    4. The chores are unpleasant.

_____

_____

Practice 2 Unit 1, "How Do You Say . . .?," page 7

A. (Paragraph 2)

    1. I had taken some classes.

    2. The classes were language classes.

    3. The classes were Japanese.

    4. The classes were before I arrived in Japan.

_____

_____

B. (Paragraph 4)

    1. Just then, I saw someone.

    2. He was one of my students.

    3. He was in the parking lot.

_____

_____

C. (Paragraph 5)

    1. The woman was old and petite.

    2. She said something.

    3. She said it in Japanese.

    4. She raced to the far right side of the store.

_____

_____

D. (Paragraph 6)

    1. I was standing in front of something.

    2. It was a display.

    3. It was the *flower* display.

    4. It was not the *flour* display.

_____

_____

Practice 3 Unit 1, "The Urban and Rural Divide," page 11

A. (Paragraph 2)

    1. The situation is just the opposite.

    2. The situation is in a town.

    3. The situation is often.

    4. The town is small.

_____

_____

B. (Paragraph 4)

    1. It is rare to find things there.

    2. The things are museums or restaurants.

    3. The restaurants are exotic.

_____

_____

C. (Paragraph 4)

    1. Finally, people might be disappointed.

    2. These people enjoy shopping.

    3. They are disappointed in the number of stores.

    4. The number of stores is small.

_____

_____

D. (Paragraph 5)

    1. Other differences exist, too.

    2. The differences are important.

    3. None of the differences makes one place better than the other.

_____

_____

Practice 4 Unit 1, "Cancer Risks," page 13

A. (Paragraph 2)

    1. However, eating foods can increase a person's chance for some kinds of disease.

    2. The foods are fatty.

    3. The disease is cancer.

_____

_____

B. (Paragraph 3)

    1. The diet must be in conjunction with exercise.

    2. The diet is improved.

    3. The exercise is regular.

_____

_____

C. (Paragraph 3)

    1. People had jobs.

    2. The jobs required more labor.

    3. The labor was physical.

    4. All this information is additional.

    _____

    _____

D. (Paragraph 4)

    1. Sunburn damages the skin.

    2. Repeated damage may lead to cancer.

    3. The cancer is of the skin.

    4. This can happen later in life.

    _____

    _____

Practice 5 Unit 1, "An Alternative to University Education," page 15

A. (Paragraph 1)

    1. A diploma is not the end of many people's education.

    2. The diploma is from high school.

    3. This happens these days.

    _____

    _____

B. (Paragraph 1)

    1. Making this choice requires a great deal of thought.

    2. This choice is difficult.

    3. The thought is careful.

    _____

    _____

C. (Paragraph 3)

    1. Going to a university requires high school graduates to live far from home.

    2. This happens often.

    3. The students have graduated recently.

    4. Many of the graduates are reluctant to live far from home.

    _____

    _____

D. (Paragraph 4)

    1. A campus offers a large variety of sports events and social activities.

    2. The campus is at a university.

    3. Students can easily become distracted.

    4. The distractions are related to their studies.

    _____

    _____

Practice 6 Unit 1, "No More Mandatory Retirement," page 23

A. (Paragraph 1)

    1. People retire from their jobs.

    2. This happens when they reach a certain age.

    3. The age is 65.

    4. This happens traditionally.

    _____

    _____

B. (Paragraph 3)

    1. There is a belief.

    2. This belief is nothing but a misconception.

    3. This belief is common.

    4. The belief is that a person's mind slows down after a certain age.

    _____

    _____

C. (Paragraph 5)

    1. They are worried about something.

    2. If older workers are allowed to continue in their jobs, something will happen.

    3. There will not be enough openings.

    4. The openings are for younger people.

_____

_____

D. (Paragraph 6)

    1. In conclusion, the age of retirement should be decided by an individual's need.

    2. The need is economic.

    3. It should also be decided by an individual's health status.

    4. It should also be decided by an individual's personal preference.

_____

_____

Practice 7 Unit 1, "The Truth about Coaches and Business Managers," page 26

A. (Paragraph 2)

    1. Coaches are responsible for training their athletes.

    2. Coaches are responsible for focusing on each individual.

    3. The individual has strengths.

    4. The individual has weaknesses.

_____

_____

B. (Paragraph 3)

    1. Athletes tend to be very competitive.

    2. This competitiveness leads to arguments.

    3. This happens often.

    4. This happens in practice and during games.

_____

_____

C. (Paragraph 3)

1. Managers know that teamwork is vital.

2. It is vital to productivity.

3. They are trained to make sure that the workplace runs smoothly.

_____

_____

D. (Paragraph 4)

1. They write up reports to keep the owners informed about information.

2. The information is about who is doing well.

3. The information is about who is injured.

4. The information is about who is not performing up to par.

_____

_____

Practice 8 Unit 2, "Frustration at the Airport," page 41

A. (Paragraph 2)

1. This was my first visit to the airport.

2. It was the international section.

3. Nothing was familiar.

_____

_____

B. (Paragraph 3)

1. I tried to ask a businessman for help.

2. He was passing.

3. All my words came out wrong.

_____

_____

C. (Paragraph 5)

    1. Tears formed in my eyes.

    2. I saw the lobby.

    3. It was deserted.

    4. I realized that I would miss my airplane.

_____

_____

D. (Paragraph 5)

    1. He smiled.

    2. It was a kind smile.

    3. He took me by the hand.

    4. He led me down a long hallway.

_____

_____

Practice 9 Unit 2, "Making Your Own Luck," page 45

A. (Paragraph 1)

    1. I did not believe it.

    2. I threw the piece of paper away.

    3. The paper was silly.

    4. I threw it in the garbage.

_____

_____

B. (Paragraph 2)

    1. I woke up the next morning.

    2. I was surprised to find something.

    3. I had overslept.

    4. I would be late for work.

_____

_____

C. (Paragraph 4)

   1. I arrived at work.

   2. I found a note.

   3. It was on my desk.

   4. It was from my boss.

   _____

   _____

D. (Paragraph 5)

   1. I rushed to the garbage can.

   2. I dug around for the chain letter.

   3. It was the letter I had thrown away the day before.

   _____

   _____

Practice 10 Unit 2, "A Little Bit of Rest," page 47

   A. (Paragraph 2)

   1. He loves to ride his mountain bike to get his daily workout.

   2. It is bright.

   3. It is red.

   4. He rides it in the hills outside of our town.

   _____

   _____

   B. (Paragraph 2)

   1. The trails are very muddy.

   2. The trails are dangerous.

   3. They are dangerous when it rains.

   4. He did not let that stop him.

   _____

   _____

C. (Paragraph 3)

    1. After that, Mohayed saw the doctor.

    2. The doctor said something.

    3. He said that he was lucky.

_____

_____

D. (Paragraph 4)

    1. He was walking along.

    2. At the same time, he tripped on the sidewalk.

    3. The sidewalk was uneven.

    4. He lost his balance.

_____

_____

Practice 11 Unit 2, "Learning to Drive," page 50

A. (Paragraph 3)

    1. My father asked me to turn on the car.

    2. He proceeded to guide me.

    3. He guided me into reverse.

_____

_____

B. (Paragraph 4)

    1. My father navigated me.

    2. He directed me around the block.

    3. This happened again and again.

_____

_____

C. (Paragraph 5)

   1. I was flying.

   2. I was in the minivan.

   3. It was old.

   _____

   _____

D. (Paragraph 5)

   1. All the information leaked out.

   2. I had learned this information in the previous weeks.

   3. The leak was out of my brain.

   _____

   _____

Practice 12 Unit 3, "Not as Different as You Think," page 65

A. (Paragraph 2)

   1. Brazil's weather varies greatly.

   2. This is because of the large size of Brazil.

   3. These variations occur from one area to another.

   _____

   _____

B. (Paragraph 3)

   1. Brazil was colonized.

   2. The colonists were Europeans.

   3. Brazil's culture has been influenced by this fact.

   4. The influence has been great.

   _____

   _____

C. (Paragraph 3)

    1. There is a mixture of cultures.

    2. There is a mixture of customs.

    3. The mixture has worked to form something.

    4. The result is ethnically rich cultures in both countries.

_____

_____

D. (Paragraph 4)

    1. Citizens believe that they have the right.

    2. They can do whatever they desire.

    3. They can be whatever they desire.

    4. This right exists as long as they do not hurt others.

_____

_____

Practice 13 Unit 3, "Transportation Decisions for Families," page 70

A. (Paragraph 1)

    1. Transportation is different from the way it was in the past.

    2. It is much different today.

    3. The past was 50 years ago.

_____

_____

B. (Paragraph 1)

    1. A buyer can compare these car types.

    2. There are two types of cars.

    3. They are compared in terms of overall cost.

    4. They are compared in terms of convenience.

    5. They are compared in terms of style.

    6. A buyer compares in order to reach a decision.

_____

_____

C. (Paragraph 5)

    1. All cars are used for transportation.

    2. However, it is important to remember something.

    3. There are differences depending on the car category.

    4. The differences are in cost.

    5. The differences are in convenience.

    6. The differences are in style.

_____

_____

D. (Paragraph 5)

    1. Choosing between two cars is a decision.

    2. The cars are an SUV and a four-door sedan.

    3. The decision is personal.

    4. The decision is for you.

    5. The decision is for your family.

_____

_____

Practice 14 Unit 3, "Higher Education Reforms in Taiwan," page 73

A. (Paragraph 1)

    1. The changes focused on steps.

    2. The steps were to enter a Taiwanese university.

    3. The steps were needed.

_____

_____

B. (Paragraph 3)

    1. A Taiwanese student today can be evaluated on his or her activities from high school.

    2. These are outside activities.

    3. These activities are not just his or her academic achievements.

    4. These activities and achievements are from high school.

_____

_____

C. (Paragraph 4)

    1. Admissions offices can prepare their own unique examinations.

    2. They can develop special projects.

    3. The students complete these projects.

    4. Admissions offices can even accept letters of recommendation.

    5. The letters are from high schools.

_____

_____

D. (Paragraph 4)

    1. Universities have the authority.

    2. They have the authority now.

    3. They can decide how they will assess their students.

    4. The students are prospective.

_____

_____

Practice 15 Unit 4, "The Truth behind Lying," page 86

A. (Paragraph 1)

    1. The celebrated story of Pinocchio teaches us the importance of something.

    2. He begins life as a puppet.

    3. It is important to tell the truth.

_____

_____

B. (Paragraph 3)

    1. There is another reason people lie.

    2. People lie to get out of situations.

    3. They do not want to be in these situations.

    4. They cannot manage these situations.

_____

_____

C. (Paragraph 5)

    1. In this situation, lying can prevent some things.

    2. The lying is protective.

    3. The lying can prevent harm.

    4. The lying can prevent disaster.

_____

_____

D. (Paragraph 6)

    1. People lie for many reasons.

    2. The reasons are good.

    3. The reasons are bad.

_____

_____

Practice 16 Unit 4, "The Fall," page 88

A. (Paragraph 1)

    1. Tensions between two groups were high.

    2. The two groups were the Western countries and the Soviet Union.

    3. The world felt a potential danger.

    4. The danger was of a disastrous conflict.

_____

_____

B. (Paragraph 2)

    1. One of the most obvious changes has been the shift.

    2. Changes occurred in the post-communist world.

    3. The shift is to a market economy.

    _____

    _____

C. (Paragraph 3)

    1. These republics are in a process.

    2. This process is current.

    3. They are shaping their identities.

    4. Their identities are their own.

    5. Their identities are independent.

    _____

    _____

D. (Paragraph 4)

    1. They do not want to be repatriated to lands.

    2. The lands are distant.

    3. There are lands such as North Korea or China.

    _____

    _____

Practice 17 Unit 4, "Television at Its Worst," page 94

A. (Paragraph 1)

    1. Mr. Stevenson has just come home from somewhere.

    2. He came from work.

    3. He had a terribly tiring day there.

    _____

    _____

B. (Paragraph 1)

1. People use television for some reasons.

2. They use television to relax.

3. They use television to forget about troubles.

4. The troubles occur daily.

_____

_____

C. (Paragraph 3)

1. There is another problem with TV watching.

2. It may cause children to have difficulty distinguishing between some things.

3. They do not know what is real.

4. They do not know what is not real.

_____

_____

D. (Paragraph 5)

1. Television has changed over the years.

2. It now includes more and more programs.

3. These programs are inappropriate for children.

_____

_____

Practice 18 Unit 4, "Effects of Computers on Higher Education," page 96

A. (Paragraph 1)

1. Individuals have created conveniences.

2. These individuals were industrious.

3. They have done this continuously.

4. They have done this to make life easier.

5. They have done this through the ages.

_____

_____

B. (Paragraph 2)

1. They are now able to sit down in front of a screen.

2. The screen is digital.

3. They can listen to a lecture.

4. The lecture is being given at another university.

_____

_____

C. (Paragraph 3)

1. It is now extremely easy to use the Internet.

2. It is now extremely easy to use databases.

3. All one has to do is type in a few key words.

4. One has to wait a few moments.

_____

_____

D. (Paragraph 4)

1. Assignments are becoming more common.

2. They are e-mail assignments.

3. They occur at universities.

_____

_____

Practice 19 Unit 5, "The School Uniform Question," page 110

A. (Paragraph 1)

1. Most people believe in the right to express their opinion.

2. The opinion is their own.

3. They do not have fear.

4. The fear is punishment.

_____

_____

B. (Paragraph 3)

    1. Uniforms give students a message.

    2. School is a special place.

    3. It is a place used for learning.

_____

_____

C. (Paragraph 4)

    1. Students' standards of living differ.

    2. The differences are great.

    3. The differences occur from family to family.

    4. Some people are well-off.

    5. Others are not well-off.

_____

_____

D. (Paragraph 6)

    1. Studies show something about students when they wear uniforms.

    2. Students learn better.

    3. Students act more responsibly.

_____

_____

Practice 20 Unit 5, "No More Guns," page 116

A. (Paragraph 1)

    1. The year was 1774.

    2. It was a pivotal year.

    3. It involved history.

    4. The history was about the United States.

_____

_____

B. (Paragraph 1)

    1. The United States has one of the largest military forces in the world.

    2. Americans are no longer called upon to use weapons.

    3. The weapons are their own.

    4. The weapons are used in the military.

_____

_____

C. (Paragraph 5)

    1. Some people say something.

    2. They feel safer having a gun.

    3. The gun is at home.

_____

_____

D. (Paragraph 6)

    1. There are statistics.

    2. They show that the occurrence of crime is much lower in countries.

    3. The crime is violent.

    4. The countries do not allow citizens to carry weapons.

_____

_____

Practice 21 Unit 5, "Life or Death?," page 119

A. (Paragraph 1)

    1. This question has been asked many times.

    2. People are not in agreement.

    3. The answer is about the punishment.

    4. The punishment is ultimate.

_____

_____

B. (Paragraph 3)

    1. There is a second reason.

    2. It involves preserving capital punishment.

    3. The reason is financial.

_____

_____

C. (Paragraph 3)

    1. These criminals do not work.

    2. They receive housing.

    3. They receive food.

    4. These things are free.

_____

_____

D. (Paragraph 6)

    1. There are many reasons.

    2. The reasons are good.

    3. The reasons are to preserve punishment.

    4. The punishment is capital.

_____

_____

Appendix 2
Peer Editing Sheets

Peer Editing Sheet 1 Unit 2, Activity 13, page 60
Narrative Essay Outline

Writer: _____ Date: _____

Peer Editor: _____

Topic: _____

1. Is the hook interesting? _____ If not, how could it be made more interesting? _____

   _____

2. How many paragraphs are going to be in the essay? _____

3. What action or event does each topic sentence show?

   Paragraph 1: _____

   Paragraph 2: _____

   Paragraph 3: _____

   Paragraph 4: _____

   Paragraph 5: _____

4. Is there a good ending to the action of the story? _____ If not, can you suggest a change to

   the ending? _____

5. What kind of ending will the story have—a moral, prediction, or revelation?

   _____

6. Do you think this essay will have enough information? _____ Does the story leave out

   anything important? Write suggestions here. _____

   _____

7. The best part of the outline is _____

   _____

8. Questions I still have about the outline: _____

   _____

Peer Editing Sheet 2 Unit 2, Activity 15, page 60
Narrative Essay

Writer: _____ Date: _____

Peer Editor: _____

Essay Title: _____

1. What are the three most memorable details in the essay? (Do not look back at the essay.)

    a. _____

    b. _____

    c. _____

2. Identify the hook. Is it effective? _____ Make any suggestions here. _____

    _____

3. What is the main point or thesis? _____

    _____

4. Reread the essay and underline all the connectors that you can find. Does the writer use them

    correctly? _____ Circle any connectors that are incorrect.

5. Is the story in chronological order? _____ If necessary, make any suggestions for changes to

    the order of events. _____

    _____

    _____

6. Does the essay have sentence variety? _____ If not, mark the sentences that could be varied or

    make some suggestions for sentence variety. _____

    _____

    _____

7. What verb tense does the writer mainly use? _____ Is this tense used throughout the essay? _____ If not, are the different tenses necessary or should they be changed? Use a highlighter to mark all unnecessary changes in tense.

8. Does the conclusion effectively end the action? _____ If not, write a few suggestions for a better ending. _____

_____

Writer: _____ Date: _____

Peer Editor: _____

Topic: _____

1. Is the thesis statement clear? _____ If not, make suggestions for changes. _____

   _____

2. Does the writer use the block or the point-by-point method of organization? _____

   Is this method effective for the subject? _____ If not, make suggestions for changes.

   _____

3. Does each topic sentence clearly state the point of comparison? _____ If not, make suggestions

   for improvement. _____

   _____

4. Do these two subjects have enough similarities and/or differences for a good comparison essay?

   _____ If not, why not? _____

   _____

5. The best part of the outline is _____

   _____

6. Questions I still have about the outline: _____

   _____

Peer Editing Sheet 4 Unit 3, Activity 12, page 82
Comparison Essay

Writer: _____ Date: _____

Peer Editor: _____

Essay Title: _____

1. In a few words, what is the essay about? _____

   _____

2. Identify the hook. Is it effective? _____ Make any suggestions here. _____

   _____

3. Does each body paragraph contain a clear topic sentence? _____ If not, underline any sections

   that need improvement.

4. What method of organization does the writer use? _____ List the main

   points that the writer compares. _____

   _____

5. Are the comparisons supported with examples? (Ask *Who? What? Where? When? Why?* and *How?*)

   _____ If not, put a star (*) next to the places that need supporting information.

6. Does the writer use connectors correctly? _____ If not, circle any incorrect connectors or any

   places that need connectors.

7. Does the writer restate the thesis in the conclusion? _____ If not, bring this to the attention of

   the writer.

8. In the conclusion, does the writer offer an opinion or a suggestion about the two subjects?

   _____ Do you agree with the writer's final words? _____ If not, why not?

   _____

Peer Editing Sheet 5 Unit 4, Activity 13, page 106
Cause-Effect Essay Outline

Writer: _____ Date: _____

Peer Editor: _____

Topic: _____

1. What kind of essay will this be—a focus-on-causes essay or a focus-on-effects essay? _____
_____ Can you tell this from the thesis statement? _____ If not, what changes can you
suggest to make the purpose of the essay clearer? _____
_____

2. Read the topic sentence for each body paragraph. Is it related to the thesis? _____ If not, mark
the topic sentences that need more work.

3. Do the supporting details relate to the topic sentences? _____ If not, which paragraph(s) need
to be developed further? _____

4. The best part of the outline is _____
_____

5. Questions I still have about the outline: _____
_____

Peer Editing Sheet 6 Unit 4, Activity 15, page 106
Cause-Effect Essay

Writer: _____ Date: _____

Peer Editor: _____

Essay Title: _____

1. In a few words, what is the essay about? _____

_____

2. Reread the introductory paragraph. Do the ideas progress smoothly from the hook to the

thesis statement? _____ If not, what suggestions for changes would you make to the

writer? _____

_____

3. Do all the topic sentences support the thesis statement? _____ Mark any that do not and write

the reason. _____

_____

_____

4. Look at the supporting details in each paragraph. Are they related to the topic sentence? _____

If not, underline the details that need revision.

5. Check the connectors in the essay. Is it easy to understand the connection between the causes and

effects? _____ If not, what is missing or needs to be changed? _____

_____

6. As you reread the essay, check for wordiness. Circle any examples that you find and suggest a way

to eliminate the wordiness. _____

_____

7. Does the writer restate the thesis in the conclusion? _____ If not, bring this to the attention of the writer.

8. Compare the introduction and conclusion paragraphs. Can you see logical connections between the two? _____ If not, why not? What suggestions for improvement can you make? _____

_____

_____

Peer Editing Sheet 7 Unit 5, Activity 11, page 128
Argumentative Essay Outline

Writer: _____ Date: _____

Peer Editor: _____

Topic: _____

If the answer to any of these questions is *No*, tell the writer why and make any suggestions for improvement that you can think of.

1. Is the hook interesting? In other words, does it catch the reader's attention?   Yes   No

2. Is the writer's opinion clear in the thesis statement?   Yes   No

3. Do the topic sentences in the body paragraphs support the thesis?   Yes   No

4. In each paragraph, do the supporting details relate to the topic sentence?   Yes   No

5. Are the counterargument and refutation strong?   Yes   No

6. Does the writer restate the thesis in the conclusion?   Yes   No

7. The best part of the outline is _____

_____

8. Questions I still have about the outline: _____

_____

Peer Editing Sheet 8 Unit 5, Activity 13, page 128
Argumentative Essay

Writer: _____ Date: _____

Peer Editor: _____

Essay Title: _____

1. In a few words, what is the essay about? _____
   _____

2. Reread the introductory paragraph. Do the ideas progress smoothly from the hook to the
   thesis statement? _____ If not, what suggestions for changes would you make to the
   writer? _____
   _____

3. Do all the topic sentences support the thesis statement? _____ Mark any that do not and write
   the reason. _____
   _____
   _____

4. Look at the supporting details in each paragraph. Are they related to the topic sentence? _____
   If not, underline the details that need revision.

5. Underline any modals. Are *must, had better,* or *should* used correctly to assert a point? _____
   Are *may, might, could, can,* or *would* used correctly to acknowledge an opposing opinion? _____
   Make suggestions for changes where necessary.

6. Reread the essay and look for any faulty logic. If you find any examples, write them here and suggest
   a way to eliminate the faulty logic. _____
   _____
   _____

7. Find the paragraph that contains the counterargument and refutation. Is the counterargument stated clearly? _____ Is the refutation strong? _____ Does it make another point in support of the writer's argument? _____ If necessary, suggest changes to the writer to make the counterargument and refutation more effective.

8. Review the essay for specific information, such as quotes, dates, and statistics. Did the writer give the source of this information in the essay? _____ If not, highlight those areas on the writer's draft and write "Need Citation!"

9. Is the conclusion effective, that is, does it restate the thesis and the writer's opinion? _____ If not, how can the conclusion be improved? _____
   _____

Index

Photo Credits